English In motion

4

Student's Book

Robert Campbell
Gill Holley
Rob Metcalf

Richmond PUBLISHING

Contents

WELCOME

Friends and school

1 Complete the questions. Then answer them.

1 Who *are* your best friends?
My best friends are Dani, Monica and Hugo.
2 What … they like?
3 Where … your English teacher from?
4 How … your teacher travel to school?
5 What … your favourite school subject?
6 Why … you like it?

At home

2 Match the verbs with the jobs.

1 – d

1	do	a	your room
2	iron	b	your bed
3	lay	c	the table
4	tidy	d	the washing-up
5	make	e	the rubbish
6	take out	f	your clothes

3 How often do you do the jobs?

I do the washing-up once or twice a week.

often sometimes usually occasionally
hardly ever never every weekend
once or twice a week three times a week

4 Who usually does each job?

My dad usually does the washing-up.

Your day

5 Write *how much* or *how many*. Then answer the questions.

In an average day, …
1 *how many* text messages do you send?
2 … exercise do you do?
3 … vegetables do you eat?
4 … water do you drink?
5 … homework do you do?
6 … hours do you spend watching TV?

Your interests

6 Write complete questions using the present simple or present continuous. Then answer the questions.

1 what music / you / listen to / these days ?
What music are you listening to these days?
2 how often / you / go / to the cinema ?
3 you / read / a book / at the moment ?
4 you / like / any TV programmes these days ?
5 where / you / usually / meet / your friends ?
6 how many / computer games / you / own ?

My Portfolio Page 11

Your attitudes

7 Complete the sentences.

1 I love *my cat.*
2 I believe in …
3 I think people should …
4 I don't understand …
5 I want to be …
6 I can't stand …

Last summer

8 Write questions in the past using the verbs.

climb fall have make
swim travel ~~visit~~ watch

1 anywhere exciting
Did you visit anywhere exciting?
2 in the sea
3 some new friends
4 a party
5 in love with anybody
6 a mountain
7 anything interesting on TV
8 by plane

9 Write about your summer and answer the questions in exercise 8.

I went to the beach this summer. It wasn't very exciting, but I …

Pronunciation

Past simple: regular verbs

10 Listen and write the past simple verbs in the lists.

/d/ *enjoyed*
/t/
/ɪd/

11 Listen and repeat the sentences.

Compare

12 Show your answer to question 6 to a partner. Find three things you have in common. Do you think you are representative of your generation?

A *We both go to the cinema once a week.*
B *That's one thing. What else do we have in common?*

ENGLISH YOU NEED – Improve your learning

1 Which students do you identify with?

2 Match the statements with the expert's advice. Then listen and check.

Daniel – C

A 'It's good to study grammar, but vocabulary is also very important for communication. When you learn new grammar, you need to use it again and again. It's necessary to practise familiar grammar, as well as learn new grammar.'

B 'Some people enjoy communicating and aren't afraid of making mistakes. Others prefer to listen more. Both are good ways to learn. But don't worry too much about making mistakes when you speak.'

C 'A lot of people think they're bad at languages and stop trying. Think positively. Use all the opportunities you have to practise English and don't be afraid to make mistakes. You'll notice the difference.'

D 'Some people think translation stops you thinking in English. Other people think it's a useful way to explain new language. Remember it isn't always necessary to translate every word.'

3 What do you think about learning English?

4 In pairs, look at your statements and give advice.

A *I need more listening practice.*
B *You should use the CD at home after class.*

1 PERFORMING ARTS

Vocabulary
- Performing arts
- Musical instruments

Grammar
- like + *-ing* form
- prepositions + *-ing* form
- Verbs of ambition + infinitive
- *have to*: present
- *have to*: past

Speaking
- Do an interview for a performing arts school
- Ask how someone learned something
- Be a critic

Pronunciation
- Diphthongs

Writing
- My hobby
- Connectors

VOCABULARY – Performing arts

1 Write the words related to dance, theatre and music, and the words related to all three. Listen and check. Then listen and repeat.

Dance – ballet, …

choreographer | stage | audience | conductor | ~~ballet~~ | play | audition
orchestra | performance | rehearsal | playwright | live music

Dance

Music

Theatre

2 Answer the questions.

1. Have you ever seen a dance performance, a play or live music?
   I saw some modern dance on a stage in the park.
2. Have you ever performed in front of an audience? What did you do?
3. Have you ever had an audition?
4. Which of the three performing arts would you prefer to do? Why?

My Portfolio Page 12

The Brit School

Reading

1 Match the information with the people.

Leona Lewis

Paul McCartney

Arctic Monkeys

Morcheeba

1. The most successful musician and composer in pop music history.
   Paul McCartney
2. One of the first bands to become famous because of the Internet.
3. Two brothers play in this band.
4. This singer won the reality show *The X Factor*.

2 Read about the Brit School. What connects the people in exercise 1 and the school?

a. They're all ex-students.
b. Some are ex-students and some are winners of Brit awards.
c. They're all winners of Brit awards.

3 True or false? Correct the false sentences.

1. Students have to pay to go to the school.
   False – It's free.
2. The students only study the performing arts, media, and art and design.
3. The school has good facilities for studying the performing arts and media.
4. The Brit Awards gives money to the school.
5. Each year, the Brit Awards give prizes to the best musicians in the school.

Do you like acting? Do you enjoy dancing? Are you good at DJ-ing or interested in writing? If you are, then maybe the Brit School is the place for you. And if you'd like to be involved in the performing arts but prefer working behind the scenes, the Brit School is also the place for you.

The Brit School is different from most other schools. It's Britain's only free Performing Arts and Technology School for 14 to 19-year-olds. Students at the Brit School study normal school subjects but they also learn about the performing arts, media, and art and design.

The school opened in 1991 and has its own professional theatre, dance studios and TV and radio studios.

Most of the students at the Brit School want to start a career in the performing arts. Leona Lewis, Kate Nash, Katie Melua, Adele, Luke Pritchard of The Kooks and Paul Godfrey of Morcheeba all went to the school and hoped to become famous one day. Today they're international stars.

The Brit School receives financial support from the Brit Awards, Britain's biggest music awards. Each year prizes are given to Britain's most talented musicians. Winners in recent years have included Arctic Monkeys, Paul McCartney, Mika and Adele, also a former student of the school.

In fact, former Brit School students have sold ten million albums in the UK. It's become the school for some of the biggest names in music, dance and drama.

GRAMMAR

like + -ing form

*Do you **like** acting? Do you **enjoy** dancing?*

love/like/enjoy	+ *-ing* form
don't mind	
prefer	
hate/can't stand	

1 Write true sentences about your likes and dislikes.

1 – I don't mind going to the theatre.

go to the theatre   write stories
perform in front of an audience
chat to friends   use my imagination
lie on my bed   listen to music   dance

Prepositions + -ing form

*Are you good **at** singing? Are you interested **in** writing?*

2 Write a preposition and the *-ing* form of the verb.

at   in   of   on   about

1. I'm good *at playing* (play) the violin. I'd like to play in an orchestra one day.
2. I don't like performing in public. I'm afraid … … (make) a mistake.
3. My sister's keen … … (dance), but I've got no sense of rhythm.
4. I love reading but I'm hopeless … … (write) stories.
5. I'm interested … … (learn) to be a DJ in the future.
6. A lot of my friends are serious … … (get) a job in the theatre.

Verbs of ambition + infinitive

*The students **want to start** a career in the performing arts.*
*They **hoped to become** famous.*

I	want/hope/plan/	to become famous.
	'd like/wouldn't like	

3 Write sentences about your future using these verbs.

1 – I want to become a teacher.

travel to   learn   study
work   become

4 Choose the correct option.

1 – singing

I love (1) *singing / sing* but I'm also keen on (2) *acting / to act*, so I'm studying musical theatre at the Brit School. I chose the course because in the future, I'd like (3) *performing / to perform* in musicals. We spend a lot of time rehearsing because we put on shows during the course. It's hard work, but I enjoy (4) *working / to work* as a team. When I leave school, I hope (5) *doing / to do* a course in dance and drama. I dream of (6) *playing / to play* the lead part in a West End musical one day.

GO 4 IT!

5 Write interview questions for the Brit School.

Are you good at acting?
What do you want to do in the future?

6 Interview your partner. Then swap roles. Who's the best candidate for the school?

A *Do you like performing in front of an audience?*
B *Yes, I do. I've acted in plays at school.*

MUSICIANS

VOCABULARY Musical instruments

1 Match the instruments with the pictures. Listen and check. Then listen and repeat.

1 – violin

clarinet | ~~violin~~ | flute | trombone | saxophone | cello | accordion
tambourine | trumpet | steel drums | double bass | recorder

2 Answer the questions.

1. Do you play an instrument? If not, would you like to play one? Which one?
   Yes, I do. I'm learning the guitar.
2. Which instruments do you think are the easiest and most difficult to play?
3. What's the best age to start learning an instrument?

LISTENING

3 Listen to an interview with Julian, Isabel and Zach. What instruments do they play?

4 Listen again. Write *Julian*, *Isabel* or *Zach*.

1. … learnt from a book. *Isabel*
2. …'s instrument was difficult to learn.
3. … had lessons.
4. … started learning before getting an instrument.
5. … copied songs.
6. …'s family didn't like the instrument.

5 Listen again. Write the names of the people who said these things.

1. You can play a lot of musical styles. *Isabel*
2. You can play anywhere.
3. People think it's an easy instrument to play.
4. It's important to be strong.
5. You don't need to play with other people.
6. You need somewhere to practise.

GRAMMAR

have to: present

*You **have to be** strong. You **don't have to play**.*
***Do** you **have to have** lessons?*

1 Complete the descriptions with *have to*. Then choose the instrument.

cost have practise start ~~make~~ play

A It's big, so you (**1**) *have to make* space for it. You can play different notes at the same time, so you (**2**) … with others. But it's complex. To improve, you (**3**) … between lessons. It's a *double bass / piano*.

B A first instrument (**4**) … a lot, but good ones are expensive. It's small and light, but difficult to play, so you (**5**) … lessons. To be a virtuoso, a player (**6**) … playing very young. It's a *recorder / violin*.

2 Write questions with *have to* about the instruments in exercise 1. Then answer them about a different instrument.

1 – Do you have to make space for it? No, you don't.

cost have ~~make~~ play practise start

have to: past

*I **had to find** somewhere to practise.*
*I **didn't have to go** to classes.*
***Did** you **have to practise** a lot?*

3 Match the sentences with activities. Then complete with *had to* or *didn't have to*.

swim play the double bass ride a bike ~~use a computer~~ do judo

1. It's easy. My parents *didn't have to* show me what to do. *use a computer*
2. My mum … buy me a special suit and belt.
3. I … have classes. My dad taught me at the local pool.
4. My parents … buy a van to transport it.
5. I … use two small extra wheels at first.

Pronunciation

Diphthongs

4 Copy and complete the table with the words you hear. Then listen and repeat.

/eɪ/: play	/aʊ/: how	/aɪ/: ride
bass		

5 Complete the interview. Then listen and check.

Lizzy You're a jazz pianist. (1) *Did you have to have* (you / have) special lessons?
Keith No, I (2) … Just basic piano lessons.
Lizzy So what (3) … (you / do) to learn jazz?
Keith I listened a lot and copied people.
Lizzy (4) … (you / practise) a lot?
Keith Yes, I (5) … . And I still practise a lot.
Lizzy (6) … (you / combine) jazz with a day job at first?
Keith Yes, but now I play professionally.

GO 4 IT!

6 Tell a partner two things that you learned to do.

I learned to swim and …

7 Prepare questions with *have to* about your partner's activities. Ask your partner, and then tell another student your partner's answers.

A *Did you have to have lessons?*
B *Yes, I did.*

YOUNG AUTHORS

1 Answer the questions.

1 Do you like reading? How often/when do you read?
I like reading. I always read before I go to sleep at night.
2 What's your favourite book?
3 Have you ever written …?
a a poem **b** song lyrics **c** a short story

2 Read about a book by a young author. Complete the details.

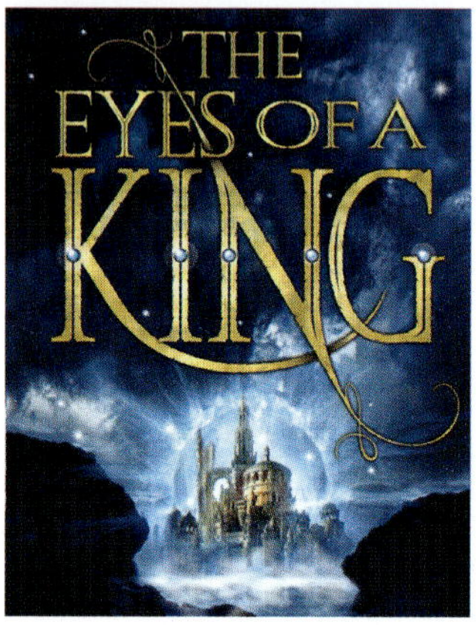

1 **Title:** *The Eyes of a King*
2 **Author: …**
3 **Publication date: …**
4 **Publisher: …**
5 **Main character: …**
6 **Genre: …**

BOOKS

When Catherine Banner published her first novel, *The Eyes of a King*, in the summer of 2008, people called her the next J.K. Rowling. Catherine was nineteen at the time but she started writing the novel when she was only fourteen.

She wrote the book in her spare time and made notes between school lessons. When she finished the book she went to a book festival in Cambridge, where she lived with her parents. She met a literary agent and asked him, 'Do you think at sixteen I'm too young to start writing seriously?'

The agent asked Catherine to send him her novel. She then signed a deal with Random House publishers.

Catherine says, 'I don't think you are ever too young to start writing if you have a story you want to tell. The most important thing that I try to do is to write about characters that I really care about.'

The Eyes of a King is the story of Leo North, a fifteen-year-old teenager living in the fictional country of Malonia. One day he finds a mysterious black book in the snow and his adventure begins.

Catherine isn't the only young fantasy writer to be compared with J.K. Rowling. Christopher Paolini started writing his *Eragon* trilogy when he was fifteen. The first part of his story about a boy and a dragon was published in 2003 and became a film in 2006.

3 Answer the questions.

1 When did the author write the book?
In her spare time and between lessons.
2 How did she find a publisher?
3 How long did it take to write the book?
4 What's the most important thing for her when she's writing?
5 Where's the story set?
6 What's it about?

4 Complete the sentences with words from the article.

1 It isn't always easy to *publish* a book.
2 A good place to see new books and meet authors is at a … .
3 A person responsible for representing an author is called a … .
4 If you're lucky, a publisher will offer you a … .
5 The people in a book are called the … .
6 A … is a story in three separate books.

Quest

- Find three more facts about *The Eyes of a King* or *Eragon*.
- Find three more facts about one of the writers.

ENGLISH YOU NEED — Be a critic

1 Listen to Mark and Sarah. Match them with the correct pictures.

2 Listen again and complete the sentences.

Mark
1 I *was expecting* it to be really boring.
2 It was … amazing.
3 I really … the music.
4 The … … about it was the choreography.

Sarah
5 … … it's great.
6 I … the *Harry Potter* books were better.
7 I … this book a little slow.
8 I … … by the ending.

3 Listen and repeat the sentences from exercise 2.

4 Complete the description with words and phrases from exercise 2. Then listen and check.

Two weeks ago I went to see the musical *Mamma Mia!* with my parents. I don't really like musicals, so I wasn't **(1)** *expecting* it to be very good, but I **(2)** … it a lot. I **(3)** … the story a little slow, but I **(4)** … the dancing was good. The **(5)** … … about it was the music, though. The songs are all by the 1970s pop group Abba, and they're **(6)** … brilliant. In fact, I bought a CD of Abba's greatest hits at the weekend.

5 Think of a book, film, concert or performance. Make notes on your opinion. Then tell a partner.

I went to see …/I read …

WRITING – My hobby

1 In pairs, answer the questions.

1 What's your main hobby?
A *What's your main hobby?*
B *My main hobby's dancing. I go to dance classes.*
2 When did you start doing it?
3 What did you have to do to learn it?
4 What are your ambitions related to the hobby?

2 Read about Julie's hobby and answer the questions in exercise 1 for her.

1 – Her main hobby's music. She plays the guitar and piano.

page 2

The Art and Sports School application

4 Tell us about one of your hobbies.

My main hobby's music. I love listening to music and going to concerts, and I play the guitar and piano. I taught myself to play the guitar about three years ago using a book, but I had to have lessons on the piano. I've had lessons since I was six.

I've always played classical music on the piano up until now, but I'm interested in learning other styles. I'd like to play jazz or blues, because then I could play in a group. My ambition in the future is to sing and write my own songs, so I'm going to have singing lessons.

Connectors

*I love listening to music **and** going to concerts.*
*I've always played classical music, **but** I'm interested in learning other styles.*
*I'd like to play jazz **or** blues, **because** then I could play in a group.*
*My ambition is to write and sing my own songs, **so** I'm going to have singing lessons.*

3 Complete the sentences with the connectors.

and ~~but~~ or because so

1 I'd love to sing in a group, *but* I haven't got a very strong voice.
2 I do a lot of exercise … you have to be fit to be good at karate.
3 I've been good at drawing … painting since I was at primary school.
4 I hope to be an actor in the future, … I've started taking acting classes.
5 I'd like to play the drums, but I don't have drums … a place to play!

Useful expressions

My main hobby's …
I taught myself to play … using …
I've always … up until now.
My ambition is to …

4 Make notes. Then write about your hobby or interest.

Paragraph 1: When did you start doing it? What did you have to do?
Paragraph 2: What are your plans and ambitions now?

5 Now read your work again. Can you find any errors?

My Portfolio Page 13

My Webpage

2 LOOKING BACK

Vocabulary
- Places in a village
- Materials

Grammar
- Past simple v. past continuous
- *used to*
- *used to:* questions

Speaking
- Tell a ghost story
- Ask about the past
- Ask permission

Pronunciation
- *used to*

Writing
- My opinion
- Adverbs

VOCABULARY Places in a village

1 Match the words with the places on the map. Listen and check. Then listen and repeat.

1 – signpost

crossroads | field | hill | wood | path | farmhouse
church | bridge | stream | fence | gate | ~~signpost~~

2 Complete the message with the words in exercise 1. Where is the meeting place? Listen and check.

When you walk to the village from the train station, you pass a (**1**) *signpost*. Then you walk across an old stone (**2**) … over a (**3**) … . Turn left and take the road through the (**4**) … . You'll come to a (**5**) … at the bottom of a (**6**) … . Go straight on. You'll see a (**7**) … to the left. The (**8**) … is in the middle of some (**9**) … on the right. Open the (**10**) … in the (**11**) … and go up the (**12**) … to the door. I'll meet you there at midnight.

My Portfolio Page 14

GHOST TOUR

READING

1 Answer the questions.

1 Do you believe in ghosts?
I don't know. I think I believe in them.

2 Have you ever seen a ghost or visited a haunted place?

2 Read the brochure. Which of these ghosts and haunted places are mentioned?

the coach and horses the gypsy the poltergeist the vicar's dog the Screaming Woods

Visit the most haunted village in England

In 1998, the Guinness Book of Records named Pluckley 'the most haunted village in England'. Each year, thousands of people visit this quiet, picturesque village, hoping to see one of its many ghosts.

The village is a one-hour train journey from London. It's particularly busy at Halloween.

Welcome. Our walking tour of Pluckley starts here at Pinnock Crossroads. Here, one cold October evening, two locals were going home when they suddenly saw a mysterious coach and horses travelling up the hill. If you listen carefully, maybe you can hear the coach approaching now ...

We are now outside the Black Horse Inn. This atmospheric pub was originally a farmhouse, and is home to the village poltergeist. One Sunday about ten years ago, while she was getting ready for opening time, the pub landlady noticed a glass moving along a shelf. Watch out! The cheeky poltergeist is also famous for hiding people's possessions.

We are now in the Screaming Woods, a particularly eerie place when the full moon starts rising behind the trees. Only a few years ago, people heard the sound of screaming while they were walking here.

Our tour ends at St Nicholas' Church. In the early 1970s a group of psychic researchers spent the night here waiting for a ghost. While they were waiting, the vicar's dog came to visit them. They didn't realize until the next morning that the vicar didn't have a dog and that the dog ... was in fact the ghost ...

3 Read again and answer the questions.

1 Why is Pluckley particularly busy at Halloween?
Because people come to see ghosts.

2 Where and when did two locals see the coach and horses?

3 What does the poltergeist do?

4 What did people hear in the woods? When?

5 Why were psychic researchers at St Nicholas' Church?

6 What did they think when they saw the dog? Were they right?

GRAMMAR Past simple v. past continuous

*Two locals **were going** home **when** they suddenly **saw** a coach.*
*People **heard** the sound of screaming **while** they **were walking**.*

1 Write *when* or *while* in the sentences.

1. I was walking along the road *when* I saw a black cat.
2. … I was looking at the cat, I heard voices behind me.
3. … I looked round, the voices suddenly stopped.
4. The cat disappeared … I was looking behind me.
5. I was feeling frightened … suddenly I felt a hand on my shoulder.
6. It was my sister. She and her friends were walking home … they decided to scare me.

2 Choose the correct option. Then listen and check.

1 – was driving

In 1997, a stranger (1) *was driving / drove* through Pluckley at about seven o'clock in the evening when the sound of horses (2) *was filling / filled* the car. There's another story about the coach and horses. This time the person (3) *wasn't driving / didn't drive* when it (4) *was happening / happened*. He (5) *was walking / walked* through the village when the coach and horses (6) *was passing / passed* in front of him. Curiously, while the coach (7) *was passing / passed*, the young man (8) *wasn't hearing / didn't hear* any sound.

3 Write the verbs in the past simple or past continuous.

I (1) *was walking* (walk) through the Screaming Woods one October morning when I (2) … (notice) that the birds (3) … (not sing) in the trees. While I (4) … (go) down the path by the church, I (5) … (see) a ghost. All the time I was looking at her, she (6) … (not move) once.

4 Write the questions. Then listen and check.

Steph Have you ever seen a ghost?
Angie Yes, I have.
Steph (1) When / it / happen?
When did it happen?
Angie About a year ago.
Steph (2) What / you / do?
Angie I was walking home from school when I saw an old woman.
Steph (3) What / she / do?
Angie She was standing at the window of an empty house. So I looked for my phone to take a picture.
Steph (4) What / she / do / while / you / look / for your phone?
Angie Nothing. She stood there, smiling at me.
Steph (5) you / feel / scared?
Angie No, I didn't. Not really.
Steph (6) you / take / a photograph?
Angie Yes, I did. Here it is.

GO 4 IT!

5 Choose one of the Pluckley ghosts. Invent the story of a meeting with the ghost.

the coach and horses   the red lady
the poltergeist   the gypsy
the vicar's dog   the Screaming Woods

1. When did it happen?
2. What were you doing?
3. What did you see/feel?
4. What did the ghost look like? What did it do?

It happened about two years ago. I was staying in Pluckley. One night I was …

6 Tell another student about your meeting with the ghost. Who has the scariest story?

A *Have you ever seen a ghost?*
B *Yes I have. I've seen the coach and horses.*
A *When did it happen?*

IN THE ATTIC

VOCABULARY – Materials

1 Match the words with the things in the picture. Listen and check. Then listen and repeat.

1 – exercise bike

drum kit ~~exercise bike~~ medal
oil painting trunk keyboard

2 Match the materials with things in the picture. Listen and check. Then listen and repeat.

1 – f

1	glass	**a**	jacket
2	leather	**b**	exercise bike
3	metal	**c**	trunk
4	plastic	**d**	scarf
5	silk	**e**	jumper
6	silver	**f**	fish tank
7	wooden	**g**	medal
8	woollen	**h**	keyboard

3 Write two more objects for each material.

1 – glass: a window, a light bulb

LISTENING

4 Tony and Richard are talking in Tony's attic. Who do you think the objects in exercise 1 belong to? Listen and check.

drum kit – Tony

Tony Tony's mum Tony's sister Tony's gran
Tony's dad Tony's great-grandad

5 Write the correct option. Then listen and check.

1 Tony's looking for *his exercise bike* / *something to take to school*. *something to take to school*
2 *There's* / *There isn't* a lot of junk in the attic.
3 Tony's father*'s got* / *had* long hair.
4 He *plays* / *played* the saxophone.
5 *Tony's parents* / *Tony and his sister* played music at Christmas.
6 His gran *sold* / *didn't sell* her paintings.

GRAMMAR

used to

*We **used to play** together when we were young.*
*She **didn't use to sell** any.*

Affirmative and negative
Subject + used to/didn't use to + infinitive
We used to/didn't use to sing.

1 Complete the description with *used to* or *didn't use to* and the verbs.

My great-grandfather was a real character. He was very independent, and he (1) *didn't use to follow* (not follow) the rules. My great-grandparents loved travelling, and they (2) … (not live) in the same place for long. I (3) … (love) listening to their stories when I was a child. My great-grandfather (4) … (wear) an old leather pilot's jacket. He was a pilot in the war, but he (5) … (not talk) about the war. He (6) … (say) that we were lucky to live in peaceful times.

2 Make true sentences with *used to, didn't use to* and the verbs.

cook   listen to   walk   send   ~~have~~   play

One hundred years ago…

1 not many people *used to have* a car.
2 people … with microwave ovens.
3 kids … or cycle to school.
4 people … the radio.
5 kids … computer games.
6 people … emails.

used to: questions

***Did** your dad **use to be** in the air force?*
***What did** he **use to play**?*

Questions				
	Did	you	use to	be a teacher?
What	did	he	use to	play?

Short answers	
Yes, I did.	No, I didn't.

3 Complete the dialogue with *used to* or a short answer. Then listen and check.

Richard (1) *Did you use to be* (you / be) in a jazz band?
Tony's dad Yes, I (2) … . Who told you that?
Richard Tony. And where (3) … (the group / play)?
Tony's dad There was a jazz club in town, and we used to play there.
Richard (4) … (you / have) a lot of fans?
Tony's dad No, we (5) …! We weren't very good.
Richard How often (6) … (you / practise)?
Tony's dad We didn't use to practise much. Just once or twice a week.

Pronunciation

used to

4 Listen and repeat the sentences from exercise 3.

GO 4 IT!

5 Write six sentences about when you were a child. Use *used to* and some of the verbs.

play   watch   collect   have (long hair, etc.)
like   wear   be

I used to play Monopoly with my family.

6 Ask another student. Find things in common.

A *Did you use to play Monopoly?*
B *Yes, I did!*
A *Who did you use to play with?*

Culture

TEENAGE BLUES

1 Decide if the sentences are about American teenagers now, in the 1940s or both?

1 Teens love fashion, music and dance.
2 Baggy trousers are fashionable for young men.
3 Teens often watch TV in the evening.
4 Girls study different things from boys at school.

2 Read a project about the history of teenagers. Check your answers for exercise 1.

Growing up used to be simple. You were a child until you were twelve and then you became an adult and started work. In the first decades of the 20th century, new laws were introduced to stop children working and extend their education. Preparing to be an adult took longer, and so the teenager was born.

The word 'teenager' was first used in the USA in the 1940s to describe a young person between the ages of thirteen and nineteen. What was it like being a teenager then? And how was it different from today?

Like now, teenagers had their own fashions, music and dances in the 1940s. The jitterbug was the first dance to encourage individual expression. And you can still see the influence of zoot suits with their baggy trousers today. Jazz was the music everyone listened to, and Cary Grant and Bette Davis were the most popular film stars.

But there were differences too. Not many people had TVs in the 1940s, so teenagers used to listen to the radio with their families. In those days, radio provided news, music and entertainment.

At school, PE was important for boys to prepare them for war. Girls learned to cook and make dresses. When the school day finished, many 1940s teenagers used to go to work. They earned money to help the family. In the 1940s, teenagers and their parents were very close – perhaps closer than today?

3 Read again. Answer the questions.

1 Why did life for teenagers change at the beginning of the 20th century?
They stopped working and education was extended.
2 When did the concept of 'teenagers' begin?
3 What music did teens listen to in the 1940s?
4 How did teenagers get music, news and entertainment at that time?
5 How was education different for boys and girls?
6 What did teens do with the money they earned in part-time jobs?

Quest

- Find out about 1940s fashion. What were 'bobby socks', a 'siren suit' and a 'fedora'?

ENGLISH YOU NEED – Ask permission

1 Look at the pictures. Who wants permission to do these things?

1 give homework in late
2 paint his room
3 go to a music festival

2 Listen to the dialogues. Match the dialogues with the pictures. Does the teenager get permission or not?

3 Listen again. Which questions do you hear?

1 Can I …? ✓
2 Is it all right if I …?
3 Is it OK with you if I …?
4 Do you mind if I …?

4 Write the responses that give permission and refuse permission.

No, you can't. ~~Yes, OK~~. I suppose so.
All right, you can if you like. I'm sorry, but no.

Give permission: *Yes, OK, …*
Refuse permission:

5 Listen and repeat the phrases from exercises 3 and 4.

6 Complete the dialogues.

Trina	Dad, do you (1) *mind* if I watch a DVD this afternoon?
Dad	No, of course not.
Trina	And can I invite some friends to watch it with me?
Dad	You can if you (2) … .
Ed	Mr Field, (3) … I give you my project on Tuesday?
Mr Field	No, you can't. You said Monday.
Ed	But I need a little more time.
Mr Field	I'm sorry, (4) … … .
Leroy	Mum, is it (5) … if I invite some friends to help me paint my room?
Mum	I (6) … so.

7 In pairs, practise and prepare the dialogues. Then swap roles and repeat.
Student A Ask for permission.
Student B Give or refuse permission.

1 You want to listen to an English song in class. Ask your teacher.
2 You want to sleep over at a friend's house on Saturday night. Ask a parent.
3 You want to arrive late for a class tomorrow. Ask a teacher.
4 You want to have a pet. Ask a parent.

WRITING – My opinion

1 In pairs, put these inventions in order of importance.

the TV   the car   the personal computer
the aeroplane   the phone

2 Read the opinion. Do you agree?

What's the greatest invention of the 20th century?

Personally, I think that the greatest invention is the phone, especially the mobile.

In the past, people didn't use to communicate so much, especially if they lived in different places. They used to write letters, but these often took a long time to arrive.

Nowadays, nearly everyone has got a phone. You can simply pick it up and speak to a person anywhere. It's made business more efficient, and improved our social lives. People can also use the phone to call for help.

For me, the phone is definitely the best invention because it's changed our lives so much.

3 Find five reasons why the writer thinks the phone is the best invention.

1 – Communication is faster now.

Adverbs

***Personally**, I think the greatest invention is the phone, **especially** the mobile.*
*Nowadays, **nearly** everyone has got a phone.*
*It's **definitely** the best invention.*

4 Match the adverbs with their synonyms.

especially   definitely   ~~nearly~~

1. Nowadays, we use the phone for practically everything. *nearly*
2. The phone is undoubtedly more important than the car.
3. Mobile phones are useful, particularly to arrange to meet your friends.

5 Write an adverb in the sentences. More than one answer is possible.

1. Today, *nearly* everyone likes travelling.
2. For me, the aeroplane is … the best invention.
3. …, I think it's more important than the car.
4. It means we can travel more, … to other countries.
5. … all airlines offer cheap flights nowadays.
6. It's … made it easier for us to meet people from other countries.

Useful expressions

In the past, people used to/didn't use to …
Nowadays, …
It's made … more …
For me, the … is the best invention because …

6 What's the greatest invention of the 20th century? Make notes. Then write your opinion.

Paragraph 1: Which is the greatest invention?
Paragraph 2: What was life like before?
Paragraph 3: How do people use it now?
Paragraph 4: Summarize your opinion.

7 Now read your work again. Can you find any errors?

My Portfolio Page 15

My Webpage

3 ON THE ROAD

Vocabulary
- Travel
- British v. American English

Grammar
- Present perfect with *just*
- *already* and *yet*
- Present perfect with *for*/*since*

Speaking
- Find out what people have done
- Interview a tourist
- Apologize

Pronunciation
- Vowel sound: /ɔː/

Writing
- My news
- Informal expressions

VOCABULARY – Travel

1 Match the phrases with the pictures. Listen and check. Then listen and repeat.

1 – plan a route

book a ticket | set off on a journey | go hiking | ~~plan a route~~ | hire a bike | stay at a youth hostel | pack a rucksack (UK)/backpack (US) | go sightseeing

2 Which things in exercise 1 do you do before travelling? Which do you do on the trip?

Before travelling: *plan a route, …*
On the trip:

3 Choose the correct option.

1. The *journey* / *travel* from New York to Chicago takes about eighteen hours.
2. We went to the USA on a school *trip* / *travel*.
3. *Travel* / *Journey* can be very expensive.

4 Answer the questions about your holidays.

1. Have you ever stayed at a youth hostel? Where do you usually stay?
   Yes, I have, in the Pyrenees.
2. Do you usually take a rucksack when you travel?
3. Do you like going sightseeing? What do you usually do on holiday?

My Portfolio Page 16

CROSS-COUNTRY USA

READING

1 Answer the questions.

1. Have you been to the USA? If not, would you like to go?
2. Which places would you like to see? Why?

2 Read the emails from the USA. Where did Anton …?

1. go sightseeing *San Francisco*
2. go on a balloon trip
3. go up a tower
4. go cycling
5. stay at a youth hostel
6. go hiking

① **Greetings from the USA!**

Hi everyone! We set off from New York two days ago. I was a bit nervous at first, but I've already made friends with a girl from Spain.
Yesterday we were in the Allegheny Mountains and today we're in Chicago. We've just been up the Sears Tower to get a view of the city. Amazing!

② **A long journey ahead**

Hi! I'm writing to you from Badlands National Park. It looks like the surface of the moon out here. We arrived this morning, and we've just been hiking. Tomorrow we're going to the west coast. It's going to be a long journey! By the way, have you received my postcard yet?

③ **I love this city!**

Hi again! Here I am in San Francisco. Today I've been sightseeing. I've visited the harbour, but I haven't been to the Golden Gate Bridge yet. I'm going to see it tomorrow. This evening Sonia and I are going to eat out in Chinatown. We're staying at a youth hostel – great after eight nights on the bus!

④ **Getting ready for home**

Hi! Since I last wrote, I've been to Yosemite Park. We hired some bikes and saw the sequoia trees. Now I'm at the Grand Canyon. I haven't seen much yet, but tomorrow we're going on a balloon trip. I've already booked my ticket to go home, but I don't want this trip to end. ☹

3 True or false? Correct the false sentences.

1. Anton didn't make any friends at the beginning of the trip.
   False – He made friends with a girl from Spain.
2. He saw a lot of trees in Badlands.
3. He slept on the bus between Badlands and San Francisco.
4. They spent a couple of days in San Francisco.
5. He saw the Grand Canyon before he wrote the email.
6. When he wrote his last email, he didn't have a ticket to go home.

GRAMMAR

Present perfect with *just*

*We've **just been** up the Sears Tower.*
*I've **just been** hiking.*

1 Write the present perfect with *just*. Where are Anton and his friends?

buy go ~~see~~ eat take walk

1 Some of my friends *have just seen* a baseball game.
2 Others … on an excursion to Universal Studios.
3 Sonia … a T-shirt on Rodeo Drive.
4 Oliver … a hamburger at Planet Hollywood.
5 Scott and I … along the Walk of Fame.
6 I … a photo of the Hollywood sign.

already and *yet*

*I've **already** made some friends.*
*I haven**'t** been to Golden Gate Bridge **yet**.*

I've **already** made some friends. (have + already + past participle)	= before now, before I expected
I have**n't** been to the bridge **yet**. (have not + past participle + yet)	= I think I'll go soon
Have you received my postcard **yet**? (have + subject + past participle + yet?)	= I think you will receive it soon

2 Choose the correct option.

1 – already

Hi,
I'm back in New York again. I've (**1**) *already / yet* found a place to stay. I haven't been up the Empire State Building (**2**) *already / yet* so I'm going there this afternoon. After that, I'm going to Central Park. I've (**3**) *already / yet* been there but I want to go again. I haven't done any rollerblading (**4**) *already / yet*! Most of my new friends have (**5**) *already / yet* left so I'm here alone. I don't want to go home (**6**) *already / yet*, but I'm looking forward to seeing you all.

3 Make true sentences with *already* or *yet*.

1 go abroad
I've already been abroad.
2 fly on a plane
3 travel on a high-speed train
4 have a holiday without my parents
5 plan my next holiday

Pronunciation

Vowel sound: /ɔː/

4 Listen and repeat the words. Then listen and repeat the sentences.

already abroad tour walk
saw tall call all

5 Write the present perfect with *just*, *already* or *yet*. Then listen and check.

Dad So, are you having a good time?
Anton Yes, I (**1**) *'ve already been* (go) to a lot of places.
Dad (**2**) … (you / visit the Grand Canyon)?
Anton Yes, I (**3**) … (come) from there. But I (**4**) … (not go / to Boston).
Dad Well, you should go. John's son (**5**) … (get back) and he says it's great.
Anton I know, Dad. You (**6**) … (tell) me twice.

GO 4 IT!

6 Prepare six questions. Use the present perfect with *yet*. Use these ideas to help you.

learn to ride a motorbike open a bank account
use a credit card read a book in English
try Chinese food join a gym/library

Have you used a credit card yet?

7 Ask a partner. Then write your results.

Marc hasn't used a credit card yet.

TRANSATLANTIC

VOCABULARY

British v. American English

1 Complete the lists of British and American English words. Listen and check. Then listen and repeat.

~~ground floor~~ | trainers | movie | underground | mobile | pants | petrol | elevator | holiday | sidewalk

British English	American English
film	(7) …
football	soccer
(1) *ground floor*	first floor
(2) …	vacation
lift	(8) …
(3) …	gas
rubbish	garbage
(4) …	sneakers
trousers	(9) …
(5) …	subway
pavement	(10) …
(6) …	cell phone

2 Complete the sentences in American English.

1 Last year I went on *vacation* to Germany.
2 I usually play … in the afternoon.
3 My sister bought some new … for running.
4 There's too much … on the streets near school.
5 Yesterday we went to see the new George Clooney … .
6 Have you ever travelled on the …?

LISTENING

3 Juliette's from the USA and Josh is from the UK. What differences do they talk about?

the weather   the people   sports   the language

4 Choose the correct option.

1 Juliette is on *vacation* / *an exchange programme*. *an exchange programme*
2 She's staying with her *friends* / *her parents' friends*.
3 She says that Britain and the USA are very *different* / *similar*.
4 She takes Josh into a *department store* / *lift*.
5 She jokes with Josh about his *trousers* / *accent*.
6 She thinks that British people are *rude* / *polite*.

GRAMMAR Present perfect with *for/since*

I've been here ***for*** *about six months.*
My parents have known them ***since*** *1995.*

1 Write *for* or *since*.

1 Juliette's studied in England *for* six months.
2 Her high school has organized academic exchange programmes … 1995.
3 Her parents haven't phoned her … a week.
4 She hasn't been back to the USA … Christmas.
5 Josh and Juliette haven't known each other … a long time.
6 Juliette's wanted to come to England … she was twelve years old.

2 Write the verbs in the present perfect and choose *for* or *since*.

I'm on an exchange programme too. I (1) *'ve been* (be) here (2) *for / since* six months with my brother. We (3) … (not have) the same experience as Juliette. She (4) … (not find) many differences here but (5) *for / since* we arrived, we (6) … (spend) a lot of time trying to understand English customs.

3 Judy's an American on holiday in Spain. Complete the dialogue. Then listen and check.

Dani How long (1) *have you been* (you / be) in Spain?
Judy For about three weeks now.
Dani (2) … (you / visit) Spain before?
Judy No, this is the first time. I'm here to learn Spanish and see the country.
Dani How long (3) … (you / want) to learn Spanish?
Judy Since I met some Spanish people in Los Angeles.
Dani (4) … (you / find) a lot of differences between here and Los Angeles?
Judy The food's better here. I (5) … (eat) lots of seafood since I arrived.
Dani (6) … (you / go) sightseeing yet?
Judy No, but I hope to go to the Prado this afternoon.

4 Complete the email. Use the present perfect or past simple of the verbs.

arrive be fly ~~meet~~ travel not learn

Hi Marc,
Guess what? I (1) *met* an American girl at a party two days ago. Her name's Judy and she's on holiday in Spain. She (2) … here for three weeks but she (3) … much Spanish yet. She (4) … in Barcelona last month and then (5) … to Oviedo. Since then she (6) … everywhere by bus and train. We're getting on really well …

GO 4 IT!

5 An American is visiting your town/city. Prepare six questions to ask him/her. Include *How long …?* and present perfect questions.

How long have you …? Have you visited …?

6 In pairs, roleplay the conversation. Then swap roles and repeat.

A *How long have you been here?*
B *I've been here for …*

Culture

TOM SAWYER

1 Answer the questions.

1 Have you ever read a book in English? If so, what was it called?
2 Have you read or seen *The Adventures of Tom Sawyer*?

2 Can you answer the questions? Read the information and check.

1 Who was the author of *The Adventures of Tom Sawyer*?
2 When was it written?
3 Where does Tom Sawyer live?

The Adventures of Tom Sawyer was written by the American author Mark Twain in 1876. It's set in the south of the USA. Tom lives next to the Mississippi River and the book describes his adventures.

3 Read an extract from a chapter of *The Adventures of Tom Sawyer*. Choose the correct chapter title.

a Huck Finn
b The Promise
c A Pirate's Life
d The Return

4 Read again. Answer the questions.

1 Why was the boat difficult to control?
Because it sometimes turned in the wrong direction.
2 What time did they arrive at the island?
3 Does Huck normally eat a lot?
4 What changes to their daily routine does Tom mention?
5 Why are the boys on the island?
6 Did they buy their food?

5 What do you think happens next? Why?

a they go home the next morning
b they live on the island for a long time
c their families find them

Everything happened as planned. Between them, the boys had brought plenty of food, which they put into the boat. Controlling the old boat was not easy – sometimes it turned in the wrong direction. But they reached the middle of the river safely and paused to look back at the town for the last time …

At about two o'clock in the morning, they landed on Jackson's Island. They made a camp just inside the forest, built a big fire and cooked a meal.

'This is the life for me!' said Joe happily.

'It's great!' said Tom.

'It suits me,' said Huck. 'I don't usually get enough to eat.'

'And we don't have to go to school or wash,' said Tom.

'What do pirates have to do?' asked Huck.

'Oh, they take ships and burn them, and get the money and hide it in a hole – usually on an island.'

Their conversation gradually died and their eyes began to close. But strangely enough, they did not sleep at once. They began to feel they might have done wrong to run away. Then they thought of the stolen food. Somehow it was different from taking an apple or a mouthful of jam. They silently decided to steal no more.

Quest

- Which states in the USA does the Mississippi River pass through?

ENGLISH YOU NEED – Apologize

1 Listen to three dialogues. Match one dialogue with the picture.

2 In which dialogue does Danny ...?

1 get drink on his T-shirt *Dialogue 3*
2 eat somebody else's food
3 arrive late
4 offer to make some food
5 say that the situation isn't a problem
6 say that he had transport problems

3 Listen and complete the extracts.

1 **Elaine** That was my lunch!
Danny I'm (1) *sorry*. I was really hungry.
Elaine What am I going to eat now?
Danny I (2) ... ...

2 **Danny** (3) ... ...
Mr Roe Just a moment, Danny. What's your excuse this time?
Danny It (4) ... ... fault. The bus broke down.

3 **Eve** Sorry!
Danny (5) ... all right.
Eve It was (6) ... .
Danny (7) ... ... about it.
Eve And (8) ... ... your T-shirt.
Danny It's OK, really.

4 Which sentences do the people use to ...?

1 apologize: *I'm sorry, ...*
2 give an explanation:
3 accept an apology:

5 Listen and repeat the sentences.

6 Complete the dialogues with these phrases.

Don't worry ~~I'm sorry~~ I'm sorry about
I'm sorry I'm I said I'm It was an
It wasn't my That's

Barry Doris. I've broken this cup. (1) *I'm sorry.*
Doris That was my favourite! I got it in Ireland!
Barry (2) ... sorry. (3) ... accident!
Doris Do you think you can repair it?

Sheila (4) ... late. The bus got stuck in traffic.
Ben (5) ... all right, I've just arrived too.

Asha (6) ... your window Mr Lee.
(7) ... fault. My brother kicked the ball.
Mr Lee (8) ... about it. These things happen. It's only a window!

7 In pairs, prepare and practise a dialogue for one of these situations.

1 You walk into somebody and his/her ice-cream falls on the ground. You apologize. He/She doesn't think it's a problem, but you offer to buy another one.
2 You've lost a friend's CD. You apologize, but he/she isn't very happy.
3 You arrive an hour late at the cinema. Your friend is waiting and the film's started. You apologize, but he's/she's angry.

WRITING – My news

1 In pairs, answer the questions.

1 How often do you write letters/postcards/ text messages/emails?

A *How often do you write letters?*

B *Never, but I write a lot of emails.*

2 Who do you write them to?

3 What do you usually write about?

2 Read the email. What does it include?

1 – thanks

an apology an invitation ~~thanks~~ questions advice congratulations good news

Hi Kyle,

Thanks for your email, and sorry it's taken me so long to reply. I've been really busy. I've just taken my motorbike driving test and passed!

How's it going? Have you started your part-time job yet? Congratulations, by the way. I hope you like it and you don't have to work too hard. Let me know how it goes.

Anyway, the reason I'm writing is to invite you to a party on the 16th. As you know, it's my birthday! I've asked quite a lot of people. Hope you can come.

That's all for now. Speak soon,
Ryan

Informal expressions

***How's it going**?*
*Congratulations, **by the way**.*
***Let me know** how it goes.*
***Anyway**, the reason I'm writing is to invite you to a party.*
***As you know**, it's my birthday.*

3 Which expression means the following?

1 I nearly forgot to say *by the way*

2 Tell me

3 I don't need to tell you

4 How are you?

5 I'm going to change to a new subject now

4 Write the expressions in the email.

Hi Maite,
(1) *How's it going?* Have you booked your ticket to Menorca yet? (2) …, I went there last year and had a great time. I'm sure you'll enjoy it. Thanks for your email (3) …, and sorry it's taken me so long to reply. I've been really busy. I'm organizing a party for my birthday. Can you come? It's on Saturday 16th. (4) … It should be fun.
(5) …, I have to go now. Mum's calling me for dinner.
Ryan

Useful expressions

Thanks for your email.
Sorry it's taken me so long to reply, but…
I've been really busy.
I hope you like it.
Hope you can come.

5 Make notes. Then write an email to a friend. Give your personal news.

Paragraph 1: Explain why you haven't replied sooner.
Paragraph 2: Ask about your friend's news.
Paragraph 3: Invite him/her to do something with you.

6 Now read your work again. Can you find any errors?

My Portfolio Page 17

My Webpage

Review A

Units 1, 2, 3

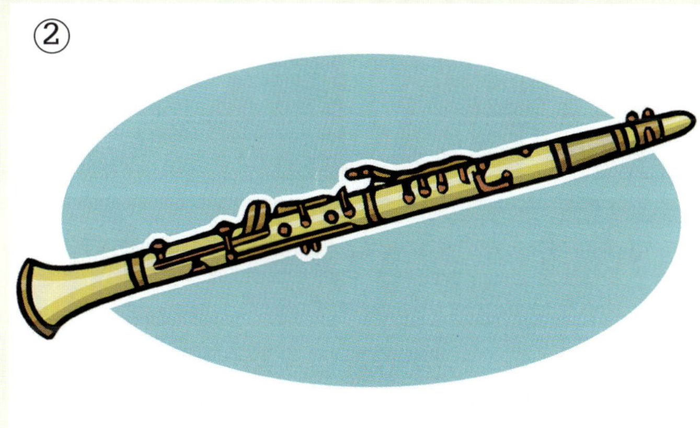

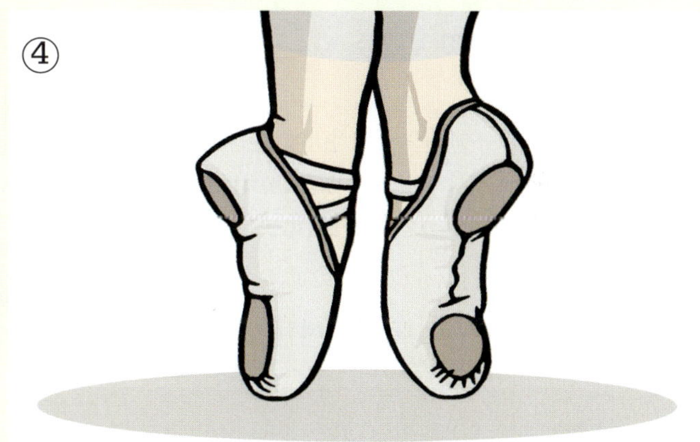

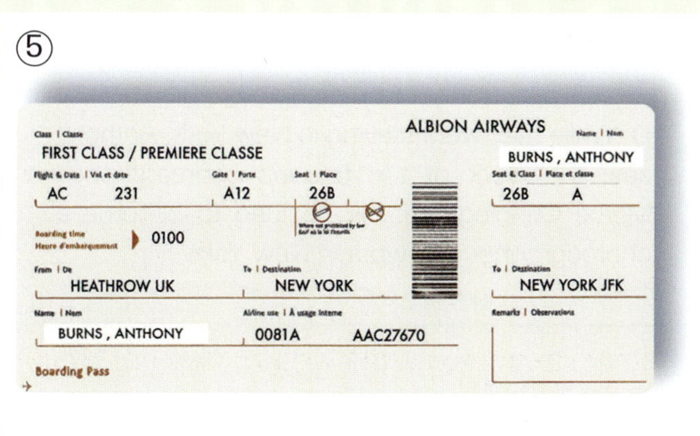

1 Match the captions with the pictures from Anthony's life.

1. My first pair. *picture 4*
2. Setting off on an adventure.
3. My lucky woollen scarf.
4. Home sweet home.
5. We are the champions!
6. Practice makes perfect music.

2 Add four more words to the lists.

Performing arts: ballet, *playwright, …*
Musical instruments: cello, …
Materials: woollen, …
Things in a village: signpost, …

3 In pairs, talk about Anthony's life.

A *I think he used to live in a village.*
B *Yes. And he played …*

MY CRAZY LIFE

READING – Dancing to success

1 Match the film titles.

1 – c

1	Billy	**a**	like Beckham
2	Bend it	**b**	Sunshine
3	Little Miss	**c**	Elliot

2 In pairs, answer the questions.

1 Have you seen any of the films?
2 What are they about?
3 Has a film ever made a big impact on you?

A *Have you seen 'Little Miss Sunshine'?*
B *Yes. It's very funny …*

3 Write the verbs in the correct tense. Then listen and check.

1 – was

Anthony Burns, the British dancer and choreographer, was born in the English village of Stone-in-Oxney in Kent in 1989. When he (1) … (be) at school, he (2) … (want) to be a professional footballer.

In 2000, while he (3) … (visit) London on holiday, his mother (4) … (take) him to the cinema to see the film *Billy Elliot*. It was while he (5) … (watch) the film that Anthony (6) … (decide) to become a dancer.

4 Put the rest of Anthony's biography in the correct order. Then listen and check.

1 – B

A He then created his own successful dance group, Burns, and went on a world tour. He was performing in China when he met music producer Al Fisher. They started working together twelve months ago, creating some of today's most famous music videos.

B Anthony studied at London's Royal Ballet School for four years. While he was studying there, he met the singer, Millie Watson. They planned a trip around the world together. Six months later they set off on a journey with just two rucksacks. They eventually arrived in the USA.

C Since last April Anthony has directed two Broadway musicals and three music videos. Last month he won three Tony Awards for his work in musical theatre. However, he still hasn't achieved his main ambition – to win an Oscar.

D While they were staying in New York, Anthony saw the work of the famous choreographer, Merce Cunningham. He decided to become a choreographer and work in New York.

5 Write true sentences about Anthony Burns. Use the present perfect and *for*, *since*, *just*, *already* or *yet*.

1 He / want / to be / a dancer / 2000
He's wanted to be a dancer since 2000.
2 He / know / Millie / they / go / to ballet school
3 He / go / to China
4 Anthony and Al / work / together / one year
5 He / win / a Tony Award
6 He / not achieve / his ambition

LISTENING – The interview

1 Put the words in order.

1 the village / what / like / was ?
What was the village like?
2 the future / any plans / do you have / for ?
3 musical / as a child / you / were ?
4 what qualities / do / a dancer / you need / to be ?
5 music / you / theatre / or / prefer / do / videos ?
6 in the streets / dance / like / use to / did / you / Billy ?

2 Listen to the radio interview and put the questions from exercise 1 in order.

1 – What was the village like?

3 Correct Anthony's answers to the questions. Then listen and check.

1 Stone isn't like a typical English village.
Stone is like a typical English village.
2 I used to play the cello.
3 I used to dance in the streets.
4 You have to be very tall to be a dancer.
5 I love the theatre because every audience is different.
6 I hope to start work on a stage musical.

4 Listen again and complete the sentences.

1 It's got a church, a pub and a *haunted house*.
2 There are a lot of … in England.
3 I didn't … practising.
4 You have to … all day every day.
5 I haven't made any films … .
6 You're wearing your lucky … .

SPEAKING

5 In pairs, think of a famous person to interview. Prepare six questions to ask.

6 Imagine one of you is a radio presenter and the other is the famous person. Ask and answer the questions.

PROJECT – Make a musical

1 *Billy Elliot* was originally a film but it then became a musical. In pairs, make a list of other musicals.

'Grease' …

2 What film would you like to convert into a musical? Choose a film and write a synopsis of the story. Include the titles of some songs to include.

3 Present your musical idea to another pair.

Our musical is 'Rocky'. It's about a boxer. One day …

SONG – Chicago

1 **Can you answer the questions? Read and check.**

1. What do singer-songwriters do?
2. When did they first become popular?
3. What are their songs often about?
4. What instruments do they typically play?

Singer-songwriter

A singer-songwriter composes the melodies, writes the lyrics and performs their own songs. The first popular singer-songwriters appeared in the 1960s and 1970s. They included Bob Dylan, Paul Simon, Joni Mitchell and Leonard Cohen.

Singer-songwriters usually write about their own experiences and often tell stories through their songs. Many singer-songwriters use either a guitar or piano to perform. Sufjan Stevens, however, is a multi-instrumentalist. This song is from the album *Illinois*. Sufjan originally hoped to make a CD for each of the American states. He hasn't finished yet! You can hear parts of the song 'Chicago' in the film *Little Miss Sunshine*.

2 **Listen to the song and answer the questions.**

1. What two places did the singer go to?
   Chicago …
2. How did he travel?
3. Who did he travel with?
4. Where did they sleep?

3 **Which adjectives would you use to describe the song? Add more.**

I think it's a very … song.
It's got a … feel.

original different laid-back commercial rebellious conventional

Sufjan Stevens

I fell in love again
all things go, all things go
drove to Chicago
all things know, all things know
we sold our clothes to the state
I don't mind, I don't mind
I made a lot of mistakes
in my mind, in my mind

Chorus
you came to take us
all things go, all things go
to recreate us
all things grow, all things grow
we had our mindset
all things know, all things know
you had to find it
all things go, all things go

I drove to New York
in a van, with my friend
we slept in parking lots
I don't mind, I don't mind
I was in love with the place
in my mind, in my mind
I made a lot of mistakes
in my mind, in my mind

Chorus

if I was crying
in the van, with my friend
it was for freedom
from myself and from the land
I made a lot of mistakes

Chorus

4 PERSUASION

Vocabulary	Grammar	Speaking	Pronunciation	Writing
• Shopping • Advertising	• Comparatives and superlatives • *(not) as … as* • *too* and *not enough* with adjectives • Sense verbs • Verbs of probability	• Do a shopping habits survey • Play the deduction game • Persuade somebody	• *as … as*	• A letter of complaint • Writing a formal letter

VOCABULARY Shopping

1 Match the words with the pictures. Listen and check. Then listen and repeat.

1 – counter

bargain | checkout | trolley | changing rooms | the sales | ~~counter~~ | receipt | basket | shopper | till

2 Complete the sentences with words from exercise 1. Are the sentences true or false for you?

1 I normally buy my clothes in *the sales* and I look for the best …s.
2 I always keep the … when I buy something in case I need to change it.
3 I don't go shopping on Saturday. There are too many other …s, and long queues at the … .
4 When I go to the supermarket, I put things in a … or a … .

My Portfolio Page 18

TEEN SHOPPERS

READING

1 Answer the questions.

1. How much money do you spend a month at the shops?
   It's difficult to say. Most months I spend about …
2. Who do you normally go shopping with, or do you go alone?
3. Do you enjoy shopping?
4. Do you buy things on the Internet?

2 Read the article and answer the questions from exercise 1 for UK teens.

1 – UK teens spend €350 a month at the shops.

How teens shop
by Hyun Tcha

Today's teenagers have got more spending power than ever. Surveys show that UK teens spend about £275 (€350) a month at the shops.

To find out their shopping habits, we followed fifteen teenagers around a London shopping centre. Our first discovery was that teen shoppers aren't as impulsive as some adults think. Teens know what they want to buy before they leave home. Most compare products online to find the best prices, and they don't buy a thing if they think it's too expensive.

Our next discovery was more predictable. Girls are more interested in shopping than boys. Surveys reveal that boys go shopping less, and spend less on clothes. The three boys in our experiment came alone, and didn't waste time. 'I don't go to ten shops to buy a pair of trainers!' Mark said.

Girls, on the other hand, *enjoy* shopping. They browse, visiting different shops to see what's on offer. They usually shop with friends, but sometimes go shopping with their parents.

What they buy is different too. Girls don't buy something if it's not original enough, whereas boys want to look like their friends. However, both boys and girls are spending more money on electrical goods and mobile phones. Shopping online is becoming more popular too. About a third of UK teens bought something online last year.

3 Read again and choose the correct option.

1 – a

1. They have got … money to spend at the shops than in the past.
   a more **b** less
2. The information about them in the article comes from … .
   a surveys **b** surveys and an experiment
3. They are … impulsive than some adults think.
   a more **b** less
4. They … carefully at the price of the things they buy.
   a look **b** don't look
5. … sometimes prefer shopping with their parents.
   a Boys **b** Girls
6. … want to wear the same clothes as their friends.
   a Boys **b** Girls

4 Find a word or phrase in the text to complete the definitions.

1. Your *spending power* is the money that you can spend at the shops. (paragraph 1)
2. If something's …, it's not surprising. (paragraph 3)
3. If you spend time in a negative way, you … it. (paragraph 3)
4. When you …, you look around shops without buying anything. (paragraph 4)

5 Make a list of the similarities and differences between teenage shoppers in the UK and your country.

Similarities	**Differences**
Like UK teens, we aren't impulsive.	*They spend more money than us.*

GRAMMAR

Comparatives and superlatives

*Girls are **more interested** in shopping **than** boys.*
*They compare products online to find **the best** prices.*

1 Complete the sentences with a comparative or superlative. Do you agree with the sentences?

1. Small shops sell *the nicest* (nice) clothes.
   I don't agree. I think that you find the nicest clothes in big shops.
2. Fashion is … (important) to girls … boys.
3. Going shopping is … (good) watching football.
4. The Internet is … (convenient) way to go shopping.
5. It's … (easy) to follow fashion … to be original.
6. Saturday afternoon is … (bad) time to go shopping.

(not) as … as …

*Teen shoppers are**n't as impulsive as** some adults think.*

2 Write true sentences with *(not) as … as* and the adjective.

1. shops / markets (cheap)
   Shops are as cheap as markets.
2. designer clothes / cheaper clothes (good)
3. a tattoo / a piercing (fashionable)
4. shirts / T-shirts (popular)
5. mobile phones / clothes (cool)
6. boys / girls (impulsive)

Pronunciation

as … as /əz/

3 Listen and repeat the sentences.

too and *not enough* with adjectives

*They won't buy something if it's **too expensive**.*
*Girls won't buy something if it is**n't original enough**.*

4 Complete the sentences with *be*, the adjective and *too* or *not enough*.

1. I don't buy designer clothes because they*'re too expensive* (expensive).
2. Teens don't shop in department stores because the clothes … (fashionable).
3. Some people think that shopping on the Internet … (dangerous).
4. I don't go into a shop if the queue to pay … (long).
5. In some clothes shops, the clothes … (big) for normal people.
6. Most teens … (old) to have a credit card.

GO 4 IT!

5 Prepare six questions about shopping habits. You can use some of the ideas below.

local shops or shopping centres markets
favourite shops go shopping buy things online
compare prices online plan shopping trips

Do you prefer local shops or shopping centres? Why?

6 Ask a partner your questions and write the answers.

7 Tell the class the results of your survey.

David prefers shopping in shopping centres because …

IT'S KWAII!

VOCABULARY – Advertising

1 Match the phrases with the pictures. Listen and check. Then listen and repeat.

1

2

3

4

5

6

- **a** give it a name and design the **logo** *3*
- **b** create an **advertising campaign** and make a **TV commercial**
- **c** **launch** and **promote** the product
- **d** write a **slogan**
- **e** do some **market research**
- **f** develop the **product**

2 Answer the questions.

1. What's your favourite fashion label? Has it got a logo? What is it?
   My favourite's Tommy Hilfiger.
2. Can you think of an example of an advertising slogan?
3. What products have been launched in the past twelve months?
4. What do you think of when you see the word 'Kwaii'?

LISTENING

3 Listen to Karen asking Annie and Ricky about a new product. Answer the questions.

1. Is Kwaii a drink, a fashion label, a car or a fragrance?
2. What type is it?
3. Do Annie and Ricky like it?

4 Are the sentences true or false? Correct the false sentences.

1. First Karen shows them the product.
   False – She shows them the name.
2. They think that the name sounds like an animal.
3. They don't think that the name is good for the product.
4. They don't immediately guess the product.
5. They try two soft drink samples.
6. They think that all the drinks taste good.

5 Complete the sentences. Then listen again and check.

~~an African word~~ car oranges cool
a new fragrance lemons

1. Ricky thinks that the name sounds like *an African word.*
2. Annie thinks that the product is … .
3. They agree that it definitely isn't the … .
4. Annie thinks that sample A tastes like … .
5. Ricky thinks that sample B smells like … and is very sweet.
6. Annie thinks that the label looks … .

GRAMMAR

Sense verbs

*It **tastes** very sweet.*
*It **looks like** the name of an animal.*

1 Write a sense verb with *like* if necessary. What's the product?

~~look~~ sound feel taste smell

1 This *looks like* the label of a shampoo bottle.
2 The name … cool. How do you spell it?
3 The fragrance is really fruity. It … lemons.
4 It … tea but it's a bit sweeter.
5 The bottle is really cold. It … ice.
6 I really like the flavour. It … delicious.

Verbs of probability

*It **might** be a new fragrance.*
*It definitely **can't** be the car.*

It **must** be the drink.	I'm sure it's the drink.
It **could/might/may** be the fragrance.	It's possible it's the fragrance.
It **can't** be the car.	I'm sure it isn't the car.

2 Choose the correct option. Then listen and check.
1 – may

Karen Now look at another name. It's Floris.
Annie It (1) *may / can't* be margarine.
Karen No, it isn't. It's a car, a fashion label or a fragrance.
Ricky Well, it's definitely not a car.
Annie No, it (2) *can't / mustn't* be a car, but it (3) *could / can* be a fashion label.
Ricky I think it (4) *might / can't* be a fragrance.
Karen Yes, it's a fragrance.
Ricky But it (5) *can't / may* be a fragrance for men. The name doesn't sound right for a man's product.
Annie No, it (6) *must / can't* be for women.
Karen You're right, it is.

3 Write *must / could / might / may* or *can't*.

1 A It isn't an animal.
B It *can't* be a cat.
2 A It isn't made of plastic.
B It … be a key ring.
3 A It's smaller than a car.
B It … be a bike.
4 A It doesn't look like a remote control.
B It … be a mobile phone.
5 A A lot of people have got one.
B It … be a watch.
6 A It's got feathers.
B It … be a bird.

4 Write sentences with verbs of probability about the places and people.

1 They don't speak Spanish there.
It could be France.
2 People often go there on holiday.
3 They speak Portuguese there.
4 It isn't in Europe.

France
Portugal
Spain
Brazil

5 He's Spanish.
6 He's got curly hair.
7 He sings really well.
8 He was in a talent show.

Enrique Iglesias
David Bisbal
Marc Anthony
Alejandro Sanz

GO 4 IT!

5 Choose an object, a person or place. Write six sentences to describe it.

It's an object. It's made of leather.

6 Tell a partner your sentences. After each sentence, they must speculate about the object, person or place.

A *It's an object. It's made of leather.*
B *It could be a jacket.*

Culture PERSUASION

1 Answer the questions.

1 How often do you go to these places?
   a fashion shops   b fast food restaurants   c supermarkets   d department stores
   I go to fashion shops but I don't often go to the supermarket.
2 What do you usually buy in them?

2 True or false? Read the article and check your answers.

1 Shops use techniques to persuade us to buy things.
2 Music, colours and smells in shops can make us spend more money.
3 Shops are designed so that we spend more time inside them.

Think before you shop!

Shops use various techniques to persuade us to buy things. The next time you go shopping, look to see how many of these tricks they use.

These days a lot of fashion shops are open at the front, making it easy for you to walk in. When you're inside, music is usually playing to make you feel relaxed. Slow music encourages you to move more slowly in a shop, and the longer you stay, the more you buy.

Notice the colour scheme. Light purple makes you feel like spending more money. Red, on the other hand, makes you feel hungry. Maybe that's why so many fast food restaurants like the colour red more than any other.

Supermarkets use more tricks than any other shop. You can often smell fresh bread or coffee when you walk in. This also makes you feel hungry and relaxed. And the everyday items you need are usually at the end of the supermarket, so that you have to pass a lot of other products before you find them.

Department stores use similar techniques. Escalators are often positioned so that you have to walk around the shop between floors. There are also few windows; the artificial light and air conditioning make you forget the outside world and spend more time and money in the store.

The list goes on. But don't worry; you can avoid falling into these traps if you think before you shop.

3 Read again. What techniques are used for the following?

1 To make customers walk into fashion shops from the street.
   The shops are open to the street.
2 To make you spend a lot of time in them.
3 To make you feel hungry in fast food restaurants.
4 To make you feel hungry and relaxed in supermarkets.
5 To make you see a lot of products in supermarkets.
6 To make you forget the outside world in department stores.

4

4 Answer the questions.

1 Have you seen any of these techniques in shops or restaurants?
Yes, I have. A lot of fashion shops play music.
2 What other techniques do shops and restaurants use?
3 Have you ever bought something that you didn't plan to buy? What?

Quest

- Supermarkets use other techniques to make you buy more. Find three more techniques.

ENGLISH YOU NEED — Persuade somebody

1 What's the best thing to say?

1 You want your mum or dad to buy you a T-shirt.

a It's good quality.
b It's very cheap.
c All my friends have got T-shirts like this.
d I'll do the washing-up for a week.

2 You want a friend to go to a party.

a It'll be fun.
b All our friends will be there.
c I won't go if you don't go.
d We don't have school the next day.

2 Listen to two dialogues. What don't the people say?

3 Listen again and complete the phrases.

1 I'm not paying £50 for a T-shirt. No *way*!
2 Please, go …!
3 I'd … to stay at home.
4 Oh … on. It'll be fun.
5 Don't be …!
6 Oh, all right then. I … in.

4 Write the phrases.

To say no: *No way!*
To persuade:
To say yes:

5 Listen and repeat the phrases.

6 Prepare and practise the following dialogues.

Student A You want a friend to go shopping with you. Persuade your friend.
Student B You don't like shopping.

Student B You want to have a piercing. Persuade your parent.
Student A You don't want your son/daughter to have a piercing.

WRITING – A letter of complaint

1 In pairs, answer the questions.

1. Have you ever bought something and then taken back to the shop?
   Yes, I have. I bought a jacket and took it back.
2. What was it? Why did you take it back?
3. Did the shop change it? Or did you get a refund?

2 Read the letter of complaint. Do you think Dylan has got a good reason to complain?

> 15 Chapel Drive
> Dorchester DT2 4NR
>
> 16th June 2009
>
> Dear Sir or Madam,
>
> I'm writing to complain about a pair of trainers I bought at your shop on High Street on 15th May.
>
> I tried the trainers on in the shop and they were fine. But when I wore them at home, they were very uncomfortable. Then I noticed that one trainer was bigger than the other.
>
> I went back to the shop, but the shop assistant refused to change them because I didn't have the receipt.
>
> It's impossible for me to wear the trainers and I think I'm entitled to a refund.
>
> I look forward to hearing from you soon.
>
> Yours faithfully,
>
> Dylan J
>
> Dylan Jones

3 Read the letter again. What information does he include?

1. the reason for the letter ✓
2. where he bought the trainers
3. when he bought them
4. the price of the trainers
5. the problem
6. the solution

Writing a formal letter

4 Match the parts of the letter with the descriptions.

1 – house number

closing expression date
Dear … ~~house number~~
city street name
writer's name postcode

	..1.. ...2...
	...3... ..4..
	.....5....
...6... ,	
...7... ,	
...8...	

5 Prepare to write a letter of complaint. Match the products with the problems.

there's a hole in it one part is missing
it's scratched it's broken it's shrunk
~~it doesn't play properly~~

1. a CD – *it doesn't play properly*
2. a sweater
3. a mobile phone

Useful expressions

I'm writing to complain about …
The shop assistant refused to change it/them …
I think I'm entitled to …
I look forward to hearing from you soon.

6 Make notes. Then write a letter of complaint.

Paragraph 1: Where and when did you buy the product?
Paragraph 2: What was the problem?
Paragraph 3: What happened when you complained in the shop?
Paragraph 4: What do you want?

7 Now read your work again. Can you find any errors?

My Portfolio Page 19

My Webpage

5 IDENTITY

Vocabulary
- Identity
- Verbs for historical events

Grammar
- Relative pronouns
- Omitting *who*, *which* and *that*
- Subject and object questions

Speaking
- Make definitions
- Create a quiz
- Express your view

Pronunciation
- Sentence stress and *that*

Writing
- My view
- Linkers of contrast and addition

VOCABULARY – Identity

1 Match the words with the things in the pictures. Listen and check. Then listen and repeat.

1 – laptop

bank account number | debit card | driving licence | fingerprint | identity card | ~~laptop~~ | password | signature | personal identification number (PIN) | user name

2 Answer the questions.

1 Which things in exercise 1 have you got?
I've got an identity card. It's in my wallet.

2 Which things have you got with you now?

My Portfolio Page 20

WHO ARE YOU?

READING

1 Read the first paragraph. What's the article about?

a A TV series
b Ways to identify people
c Ways to catch criminals

2 Read the online article. Match the headings with the paragraphs.

Eyes Fingerprints ~~DNA~~ Hand geometry Face recognition

Fans of the popular TV series *CSI: Crime Scene Investigation* will know that there are a lot of ways to identify criminals and their victims. What are these, and how reliable are they as a way of checking identity?

1 DNA
This carries the genetic information which we inherit from our parents, and is only the same in identical twins. It's highly reliable, but takes time to analyze, so it's usually only used in criminal investigations.

2 ...
Investigators have used these for identification for over 100 years. They're partly genetic and partly formed by movements that we make before we are born, so they are completely unique. They're easy to collect and analyze, and they are a reliable way of checking identity.

3 ...
This method is not very reliable because our faces don't have enough unique features. CCTV cameras in London regularly film people who have committed a crime, but the technology they use hasn't identified any criminals.

4 ...
The colour and texture of our irises are unique, and an iris scan is a quick and reliable way to identify people. For this reason it's used in places where security is a priority. A lot of airports now use iris-scanning systems.

5 ...
The shape of the hand is less unique than a fingerprint, but in low-security contexts like sports centres, hand geometry readers are a convenient way to check identity when combined with a password, card or visual identification.

3 Read the article again. Write one or two ways of identifying people.

1 It's good in high-security situations.
an iris scan
2 They're unique to every individual.
3 It works well when a second form of identity is also used.
4 It's mainly used for solving crimes.
5 They're reliable and quick and easy to use.
6 It's the least reliable.

GRAMMAR

Relative pronouns

*Cameras film people **who/that** have committed a crime.*
*It's used in places **where** security is a priority.*

People	Cameras film people **who/that** have committed a crime.
Things	DNA carries the genetic information **which/that** we inherit.
Places	It's used in places **where** security is a priority.

1 Complete the definitions with *who*, *which* or *where*. Then match them with words in the article.

1 The part of the eye *which* is coloured.
iris
2 A place … you go to catch a plane.
3 A person … has committed a crime.
4 A building … you can do different sports.
5 The mark … your finger leaves on things.
6 Two people … were born at the same time.

2 Replace *that* with *who* or *which*. Then match the definitions with the words.

seatbelt passenger suspect
~~passport~~ detective series

1 It's a document *that* you need when you travel. *which – passport*
2 It's a police officer *that* investigates crimes.
3 It's a person *that* the police have arrested.
4 It's a TV show *that* has a lot of episodes.
5 It's a person *that*'s travelling on a plane.
6 It's a thing *that* you wear in a car.

Pronunciation

Sentence stress and *that* /ðət/

3 Listen and underline the stressed words in exercise 2. Then listen and repeat.

1 – It's a <u>document</u> that you <u>need</u> when you <u>travel</u>.

Omitting *who*, *which* and *that*

DNA carries the genetic information we inherit.

Optional	The technology (**which/that**) they use hasn't identified any criminals.
Not optional	Cameras film people **who/that** have committed a crime.

4 Write definitions for the following words.

~~a tin opener~~ a stamp a pen-friend
scissors a classmate a stranger

1 – It's a thing you use to open tins.

GO 4 IT!

5 Prepare questions about these things.

languages films people jobs
objects books buildings

What do you call a film that makes people laugh?

6 Ask a partner your questions.

A *What do you call a film that makes people laugh?*
B *Is it a comedy?*

SUPERBRAIN

VOCABULARY Verbs for historical events

1 Complete the sentences. Then listen and check.

broke out | shot | attempted | ~~fought for~~ | became | beat | sank | founded

1 Americans *fought for* independence from Britain between 1775 and 1783.
2 George Mallory and Andrew Irvine ... to climb Everest in 1924.
3 Hong Kong ... part of China in 1997.
4 The French Revolution ... in 1789.
5 *The Prestige* ... off the coast of Spain in 2002, causing an environmental disaster.
6 The Spanish football team ... Germany in the Euro 2008 final.
7 Bill Gates and Paul Allen ... Microsoft in 1975.
8 Mark Chapman ... John Lennon outside his New York home in 1980.

2 Write the infinitive and the past of the verbs from exercise 1. Listen and check. Then listen and repeat.

1 – fight – fought

LISTENING

3 Listen to the quiz show SuperBrain. Kathryn answers questions on famous women in history. How many questions does she answer correctly?

4 Listen again. Answer the questions.

1 What are the contestants' specialist subjects?
2 Why was Cleopatra famous?
3 Where did Anne Frank hide from the Nazis?
4 What was Amelia Earhart doing when she disappeared?
5 How did Rosa Parks start the Civil Rights movement in the USA?
6 What did voices tell Joan of Arc?

5 Listen again. Complete the questions. Then answer the questions.

1 Which First Lady *helped* the poor and ... for women's rights in Argentina in the 1940s?
2 What ... Marie Curie ... with her husband in 1898?

6 Listen to the end of the programme and check.

GRAMMAR Subject and object questions

***Who** helped the poor? **What** did Anne Frank write?*

Subject question	Object question
Who **helped** the poor?	What **did** Anne Frank **write**?

1 Write the answers. Then choose the correct option for the question.

the White House Hannibal Valentine's Day Nobody World War II ~~1912~~

1. The *Titanic* sank in *1912*.
2. … owns the North Pole.
3. The President of the USA lives at … .
4. … broke out on 3rd September 1939.
5. People in the UK celebrate … on 14th February.
6. … rode elephants over the Alps into Italy in 218 BC.

a When *did the* Titanic *sink* / *sank the* Titanic?
When did the Titanic sink?
b Who *owns the North Pole* / *does the North Pole own*?
c Where *does the President of the USA live* / *lives the President of the* USA?
d What *did happen* / *happened* on 3rd September 1939?
e What *do people celebrate* / *celebrate people* in the UK on 14th February?
f Who *did elephants ride* / *rode elephants* over the Alps into Italy in 218 BC?

2 Write the questions. Then write the answers. Then listen and check.

1. Which American artist / sing / 'Slipping Away' with the Spanish singer Amaral ?
Which American artist sang 'Slipping Away' with the Spanish singer Amaral? – Moby
2. What / John Logie Baird / invent / in the 1920s ?
3. Where / Zulu people / come from ?
4. Who / shoot / J. F. Kennedy on 22nd November 1963 ?
5. Why / the Egyptians / build / pyramids ?
6. Who / open / the Houses of Parliament in the UK every year ?

3 Write questions that give the words in bold as answers. Use the question words in brackets.

1. **Vincent Van Gogh** cut off part of his left ear. (Who)
Who cut off part of his left ear?
2. The Olympic Games take place **every four years**. (How often)
3. Daniel Craig played **James Bond** in the film *Casino Royale*. (Who)
4. The Great Wall of China starts in **Shanhaiguan**. (Where)
5. **Martin Luther King** said, 'I have a dream …'. (Who)
6. Man first walked on the moon on **21st July 1969**. (When)

GO 4 IT!

4 Write three subject questions and three object questions. Use the verbs below to help you.

fight for invent design discover found become break out say sing beat win

Who sang the song 'Hips Don't Lie'?
What did Alexander Graham Bell invent?
Who became the president of the USA in 2008?

5 Ask a partner. How many points do they score?

A *Who sang the song 'Hips Don't Lie'?*
B *That's easy. It was Jennifer Lopez.*
A *No. It was Shakira.*

Culture THIS IS YOUR SECOND LIFE!

1 Answer the questions.

1 What's an avatar?
I think you use them on the Internet …
2 Is it difficult to create an avatar?
3 Who created Teen Second Life?
4 What is TSL?
5 Is it safe to use?

2 Read the text and match the questions from exercise 1 with the answers in the text. Then listen and check. Were your answers in exercise 1 correct?

1 – What is TSL?

3 True or false? Correct the false sentences.

1 Anyone can use TSL.
False – You have to be 13–17 years old.
2 Most avatars are mythical creatures.
3 Learning to fly in TSL is difficult.
4 Philip Rosedale created TSL when he was only ten.
5 He thought of the idea after seeing a film.
6 Using social networking sites can be dangerous.

4 Match the definitions with the words.

virtual world   residents   ~~avatar~~
social networking sites   profile   *Snow Crash*

1 A graphic version of a person. *avatar*
2 Your personal details on a website.
3 The people who exist in TSL.
4 Title of the book that inspired TSL.
5 A computer simulation of a real or imaginary place.
6 Internet sites where people can meet other people.

Quest

- Find the origin of the word avatar.

Put your questions to Alice and her avatar.

1 Pablo, Portugal: What is TSL?
Hi Pablo. It stands for Teen Second Life. It's a 3-D virtual world for teens between the ages of thirteen and seventeen where you can make friends from around the world, play games, and practise your English using an avatar.

2 Ling Ling, Singapore: …
The first thing you have to do when you go to TSL is create a graphic representation of yourself. These are called avatars. Most avatars have a human form, but many residents choose robots, animals or mythical creatures to represent them.

3 Shuet-Kei, Hong Kong: …
No, it's easy and it's fun because you can invent a totally new identity. You can choose your hair, your height and the clothes you wear. My avatar is called Amazing Grace and she's got wings. Learning how to make your avatar walk and fly isn't very easy. I walked into a lot of walls when I started using TSL.

4 Lourdes, Peru: …
Philip Rosedale. He built his first computer when he was ten and thought of the idea of a virtual world in 1991. He was inspired by a science-fiction novel called *Snow Crash*.

5 Mehmet, Turkey: …
Good question, Mehmet. It's safer than a lot of other social networking sites because it's exclusively for young people and you can create an identity. On a lot of sites you have to post your personal information and sometimes it's difficult to remove your profile.

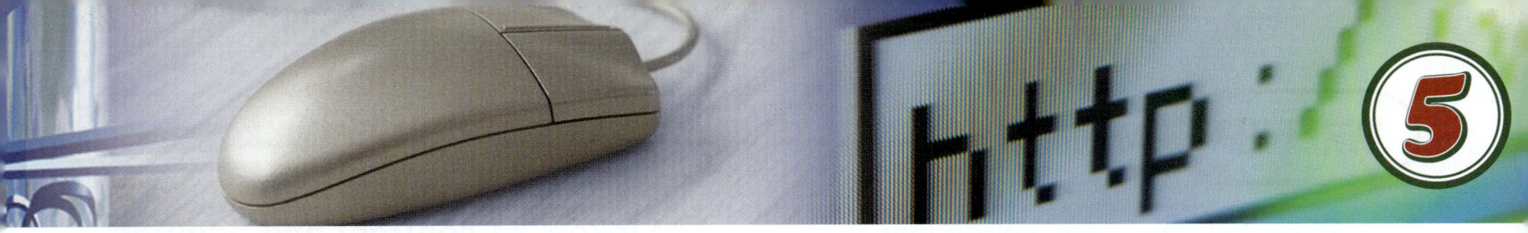

ENGLISH YOU NEED – Express your view

1 Are these words and phrases positive or negative?

1 really good *positive*
2 a waste of time
3 awful
4 brilliant
5 rubbish
6 great

2 Listen to Amanda, Jake and Josh talking about Teen Second Life. Match the opinions with the names.

1 … feels negative about TSL.
2 … doesn't feel positive or negative about TSL.
3 … feels positive about TSL.

3 Listen again. Complete these phrases.

1 I *think* it's good because you can escape into a fantasy world.
2 I don't … . In … …, it's more important to meet people in the real world.
3 Do you really … … ?
4 What … … … , Josh?
5 I … with Jake. Real life is better because it's real.
6 I … so. But you can't fly in real life, can you?

4 Put the phrases from exercise 3 in the correct category.

Give an opinion: *I think, …*
Ask for an opinion:
Agree:
Disagree:

5 Listen and repeat.

6 Complete the conversation. Then listen and check.

Dani Do you watch *CSI: Miami*?
Isabel Yes, always. What (1) *do* you *think* of it?
Dani I think it's awful.
Isabel Do you really (2) … …? I think it's brilliant.
Dani In my (3) …, it's all too predictable.
Isabel I (4) … … . There are always surprises.
Dani I (5) … the first series was better because it was more original.
Isabel Yes, I (6) … …, but I think the current series is just as entertaining.
Dani That's your opinion.

7 In pairs, discuss your opinions about one of these options. Use expressions from exercise 4.

a TV programme a film a sports match
a singer, group or album a website

A *Did you see the football match on Saturday?*
B *Yes, I did.*
A *What did you think of it?*

WRITING – My view

1 In pairs, talk about the newspaper headlines. Are they good or bad ideas? Give reasons for your opinions.

① **European schools plan to reduce summer holidays to four weeks**

A *What do you think of the first headline?*
B *I think it's bad because students need a long holiday.*

② **It will be illegal to use the Internet if you're under eighteen**

③ **Schools plan to introduce security cameras in all classes**

④ **The UK plans to introduce identity cards for the first time**

2 Read Dave's posting on an Internet forum and answer the questions.

1 Which headline is his posting about?
2 Does he have the same opinion as you?

I'm writing about plans to introduce an identity card in the UK. My dad reckons this will make the country safer. However, we've never had an ID card before, so why have one now?

What's more, the new ID card will contain information that nobody needs to know. Although my friends and I never do anything wrong, the police sometimes stop us and take our names. If we have to carry ID cards, they'll know everything else about us as well. Who needs this personal information?

For me, it's a question of personal freedom. I'm innocent, so why treat me like a criminal?

Dave, Birmingham

Linkers of contrast and addition

***However**, we've never had an identity card before.*
***What's more**, it will contain information that nobody needs to know.*
***Although** we never do anything wrong, the police sometimes stop us.*
*They'll know everything else about us **as well**.*

3 Complete with *however*, *although*, *what's more* or *as well*.

I understand why Dave from Birmingham doesn't like identity cards. (**1**) *What's more*, he's right to say that we've never needed one before. (**2**) …, a lot of people carry weapons these days. We need to stop terrorists (**3**) … . So (**4**) … it's inconvenient to carry an identity card, I think it's a good idea.

Useful expressions

I'm writing about …
… reckons …
For me, it's a question of …
… so why …?

4 Make notes. Then write to an Internet forum. Give your opinion about one of the other headlines.

Paragraph 1: Explain why you're writing. Give one reason for your opinion.
Paragraph 2: Give other reasons for your opinion.
Paragraph 3: Write your conclusion.

5 Now read your work again. Can you find any errors?

My Portfolio Page 21

My Webpage

6 CONNECT

Vocabulary
- Natural disasters
- Crime

Grammar
- Future forms
- *will* and *might*
- First conditional

Speaking
- Create a 'Youth Connect' group
- Organize a debate
- Make a presentation

Pronunciation
- Word stress and /ə/

Writing
- An argument
- Sequencing ideas

VOCABULARY – Natural disasters

1 Match the words with the pictures. Listen and check. Then listen and repeat.

1 – earthquake

flood | forest fire | desertification | iceberg | hurricane | ~~earthquake~~ | tornado | volcanic eruption | drought | glacier

2 Relate the words with places in the world.

There was a terrible hurricane in New Orleans a few years ago.

3 Answer the questions.

1 Have you ever experienced an earthquake?
Yes, I have, but only a small one.
2 Are there any forest fires where you live?
3 Has your area got any water problems – floods or droughts?

My Portfolio Page 22

YOUTH CONNECT

READING

1 Which of the following do you associate with global warming?

I think that some floods are the result of global warming.

floods forest fires desertification icebergs hurricanes earthquakes tornadoes volcanic eruptions droughts glaciers

2 Read about Youth Connect. Answer the questions.

1 Which things in exercise 1 do they talk about?
2 What other problems do they mention?

Youth Connect (YC) is a worldwide organization and will be ten years old this summer. YC connects young people who want to improve the world we share. Read what YC members are talking about today and what they're planning to do.

Hi. I'm **Aleqa** from **Greenland**. People are very concerned about what's happening here. The thickness of the Arctic glaciers is half what it was 50 years ago. We need to stop global warming now, or the glaciers will melt, sea levels will rise, and the polar bear will probably disappear!

Action Plan: We're going to hold a demonstration this month. We're meeting on Sunday 16th to organize it.

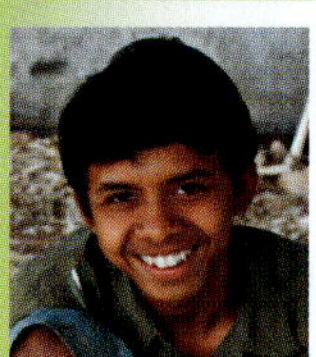

My name is **Joe Johansyah**. I live in **Denpasar, Bali**. A lot of people think that corals are plants but, in fact, they're animals – and many corals are endangered species. Corals can't live in warmer seas and the corals here probably won't survive climate change. About a quarter of the world's coral reefs have already died.

Action Plan: Next weekend, we're going to give out leaflets in Catur Muka Square.

Hi everyone. This is **Helena** in **Brazil**. Experts here say that the Amazon Rainforest will turn into a desert if we don't take action. There are more droughts here than before and without rain, the forests will die and global warming will accelerate.

Action Plan: We're travelling to Brasilia this Friday to petition the Government.

Join today and tell us what's happening where you live.

3 Read again. Is the information true or false? Correct the false sentences.

1 Youth Connect is a local organization. *False – It's worldwide.*
2 Arctic glaciers are thinner than they were in the past.
3 Corals are plants.
4 Corals won't survive because they need warmer water.
5 There is a danger of floods in the Amazon Rainforest.
6 Without the rainforests, the problem of global warming will get worse.

4 Answer the questions.

1 Which is the most serious problem? Why?
2 Which action plan is the most effective? Why?

GRAMMAR Future forms

*Youth Connect **will be** ten years old.*
*The polar bear **will probably disappear**.*
*We**'re going to hold** a demonstration.*
*We**'re meeting** on Sunday 16th to organize it.*

Future fact	Youth Connect **will be** ten years old.
Future prediction	The polar bear **will probably disappear**.
Future intention	We**'re going to hold** a demonstration.
Future plans	We**'re meeting** on Sunday 16th.

1 Write *will* or *won't* and a verb in the sentences.

find ~~cause~~ need rise affect continue

1. Global warming *will cause* a rise in temperatures all over the world.
2. Glaciers … to melt.
3. Arctic animals like polar bears … enough food.
4. Sea levels … .
5. Hurricanes and tornadoes … more countries.
6. Governments … to invest in flood protection.

2 What's your opinion? Complete the sentences with *will probably* or *probably won't* about your country.

1. Climate change *will probably* affect this country in the future.
2. Rainfall … increase here in the next few years.
3. Certain areas … suffer droughts.
4. Tourists … stop visiting this country.
5. People … be more concerned about climate change.
6. The government … do something to solve the problem.

3 Complete the dialogue with *will* or *be going to*.

Billy Global warming is really scary. I've decided that I (1) *'m going to* take action.
Lorna Don't worry. I'm sure scientists (2) … solve the problem soon.
Billy I don't think so.
Lorna But I think they (3) … build cities on the moon soon.
Billy That's not the point.
Lorna All right, so what (4) … you … to do about it?
Billy I've spoken to people at school. We (5) … organize a petition.
Lorna Yeah, right. I'm sure you (6) … forget about it next week.

4 Write about Billy's action plan. Use the present continuous.

I'm organizing a jumble sale on the 3rd.
Me organize a jumble sale – 3rd
Tara give a class presentation – 13th
All of us have a meeting on – 15th
Ken and Ada do sponsored walk – 19th
Our theatre group put on a play – 23rd
Lucy and Karen go to a conference – next month

GO 4 IT!

5 Choose a problem in your area and answer the questions.

1. What's the problem?
   There are a lot of forest fires in this area.
2. Why is it happening?
3. What are the effects of the problem?
4. What are you going to do? (Invent!)

6 Tell a partner about the problem.

I'm concerned about the problem of …

PIRATES

VOCABULARY Crime

1 Match the pictures with three of the words or phrases.

1 – shoplifter

Is it OK to ROB SOMEBODY?

To STEAL A CAR?

To BURGLE A HOUSE?

To be a SHOPLIFTER?

Buying an illegal copy of a film is a crime.

PIRACY is theft!

2 Complete the dictionary entries with *rob*, *steal* and *burgle*.

1 … (v) Take something without permission and not return it.
2 … (v) Go into a house and illegally take money or property.
3 … (v) Force a person or bank to give you money or property.

3 Complete the word families with words from the leaflet.

1 *crime* (act), criminal (person)
2 shoplifting (act), … (person)
3 … (act), thief/thieves (pl) (person)
4 … (verb), robbery (act), robber (person)
5 … (verb), burglary (act), burglar (person)
6 legal/… (adjectives), legalize (verb)

LISTENING

4 Listen to a school debate. What motion are Elsie and Sean debating?

a Downloading music and films should be legal.
b The punishment for web piracy should be prison.
c Downloading music and films should be more expensive.

5 Listen and answer the questions.

1 Who's defending the motion in the debate – Elsie or Sean? *Elsie*
2 Why does Sean think web piracy's a crime?
3 What example does Sean give to show that web piracy is theft?
4 What happens to people who share music and films in some countries?
5 Why does Sean think that illegal downloading is bad for everyone?
6 Why does Elsie think that sharing entertainment on the web is positive?

GRAMMAR

will and *might*

*It **might stop** a few people.*
*Some teenagers **will probably** go to prison.*
*It **probably won't** happen next year.*

1 Write sentences with *will probably, probably won't* and *might*. Tick (✓) the sentences that you agree with.

1. It's possible that my friends will share files online tonight.
   My friends might share files online tonight.
2. I don't believe that people will buy all their music and films in ten years' time.
3. It's probable that we'll have to pay to use the Internet in the future.
4. I can't imagine that a person in my country will go to prison for web piracy this year.
5. I think it's possible that file sharing on the Internet will be legal in ten years' time.
6. It's almost certain that DVD rental stores will exist in five years' time.

First conditional

*They **won't be able to make** films if they **don't make** any money.*
***If** people **go** to prison, it **might** stop others downloading files.*
*It **will probably** kill entertainment **if** people **continue** to download files.*

2 Match the parts of the sentences. Then write true sentences. Use the first conditional with *will, will probably, might, probably won't* or *won't*.

1. If CD sales / continue / to fall,
   If CD sales continue to fall, groups will probably sell their music directly to fans.
2. Young people / be / less healthy than their parents
3. If we / make / smoking illegal,
4. There / be / less crime
5. If advertising / not change,
6. If teachers / get / stricter,

a their students' behaviour / get / better.
b it / save / thousands of lives.
c if we / not ban / fast food.
d more girls and boys / suffer / from anorexia.
e ~~groups / sell / their music directly to fans.~~
f if we / punish / criminals more severely.

Pronunciation

Word stress and /ə/

3 Copy the words. Listen and mark the stressed syllable. Listen again and identify the /ə/ sound. Then listen and repeat.

criminal shoplifter piracy robbery legal prison Internet entertainment company probably

criminal
/ə/

GO 4 IT!

4 Organize a debate about one motion.

1. We should ban fast food.
2. Criminals should get training, not prison sentences.
3. Smoking should be illegal.
4. Everyone should stay at school until they're eighteen.
5. We don't need to ban very thin models in advertising.

5 Prepare your arguments, and then hold the debate.

Every day, thousands of people eat fast food. If we don't ban it, …

Culture

CONNECTING PEOPLE

1 Answer the questions.

1 Who are these people and what do they do?
Kevin Bacon is an actor. He was in 'Apollo 13'.

~~Kevin Bacon~~ Hillary Clinton Hilary Duff
Angelina Jolie Nicole Kidman Madonna
Camilla Parker Bowles Will Smith

2 Can you find any connections between them?

2 Read the magazine article. How are these people connected?

1 Will Smith and Kevin Bacon.
Will Smith starred in a film that inspired a game about Kevin Bacon.

2 Kevin Bacon and Nicole Kidman.

3 Hillary Clinton and Madonna.

4 Angelina Jolie and Alanis Morissette.

Six Degrees of Separation

How many people do you know? Maybe you're connected to more people than you realize. 'Six degrees of separation' is a theory that suggests that anyone on the planet can be connected to any other person through five other people.

The theory first appeared in 1929 in a short story called *Chains* but it didn't become popular until the 1990s when the film *Six Degrees of Separation*, starring Will Smith, was released.

The film inspired a game called 'Six Degrees of Kevin Bacon'. The aim of the game was to link any actor to Kevin Bacon through no more than six film connections.

The game then inspired Kevin Bacon to start a website called SixDegrees.org, a charitable social network. Bacon invited celebrities to promote their favourite charities on the site. They include Nicole Kidman (UNIFEM), Ashley Judd (YouthAIDS), Hilary Duff (Kids with a Cause) and Jessica Simpson (Operation Smile).

But the people we are most closely connected to are our family members, and finding family connections can reveal some surprising facts. According to a Washington genealogist, Hillary Clinton and Madonna are tenth cousins. They share the same great-great-great-great-great-great-great-great-great-grandparents. Clinton is also distantly related to Angelina Jolie.

When she heard the news, Clinton said, 'I am thrilled to be related to Madonna and Angelina Jolie. They're both strong independent women.' Hillary Clinton is also related to Camilla Parker Bowles, Celine Dion and Alanis Morissette! Who would you like to be related to and why?

3 Are the sentences true or false? Correct the false sentences.

1 The Six Degrees theory first appeared in the 1990s. *False – It first appeared in 1929.*
2 The theory claims we're all connected through six other people.
3 Kevin Bacon starred in the film *Six Degrees of Separation*.
4 The film title is also the name of a game.
5 SixDegrees.org is a website where famous people support charities.
6 Hillary Clinton's disappointed that she's related to Madonna.

Quest

- Imagine you are a celebrity. What charity would you like to support? Find out about the work they do.

ENGLISH YOU NEED – Make a presentation

1 Listen to Miranda, Jennifer and Billie making presentations. Put the themes in order.

a Finding out about my family
b A person I admire
c Mobiles and our health

2 Listen again and answer the questions.

1 What is Maite's job? *She's a teacher.*
2 What does Miranda say about Maite's character?
3 What did Jennifer have to become to find information?
4 Where did she look for clues?
5 What do the phone companies want us to do?
6 How do we cause environmental problems?

3 Complete the phrases. Listen and check. Then listen and repeat.

look told want ~~talk~~ mean
have like start give know

Today I'd like to (1) *talk* to you about a person I admire.
I'm going to (2) … by telling you about her character.

So, I've (3) … you about why I became interested.
Now let's (4) … at how I found information.
What does this (5) …? Well, to (6) … you an example …

To conclude, I'd (7) … to summarize the key points.
Firstly, scientists still don't (8) … the risks.
Secondly, phone companies (9) … us to spend money.
(10) … you … any questions?

4 Make a presentation about one of the options below. Make notes. Then give your presentation. Include phrases from exercise 3.

1 A person – someone famous or a person you admire.
2 A hobby – something you enjoy doing or know a lot about.
3 An issue – something you feel strongly about.

Today I'd like to talk about … I like this person because … I first met him/her …

WRITING — An argument

1 Can you think of three reasons to ban cars from town centres?

1 – To reduce pollution.

2 Read the composition and answer the questions.

1 Does the student mention your reasons from exercise 1?

2 What other reasons are given?

Cars should be banned from town centres. Do you agree?

I agree with the statement that cars should be banned from town centres.

Firstly, cars produce carbon dioxide, which contributes to global warming. If we don't reduce carbon emissions, we'll see more problems of climate change in the future.

Secondly, in towns people can cycle or walk instead of using a car. This is healthier for us. Moreover, people often drive dangerously in town centres. If we ban cars in town centres, we might reduce the number of accidents.

In conclusion, I think we should ban cars in city centres to protect our health, and the health of our planet.

Sequencing ideas

***I agree with the statement that** cars should be banned.*
***Firstly**, cars produce …*
***Secondly**, in towns … **Moreover**, people often drive dangerously.*
***In conclusion**, I think we should ban cars.*

3 Choose one of the statements and plan a composition.

Exams are a good thing.
TV has too much influence on our lives.
Teenagers should read more.

1 Decide if you agree or disagree.
2 Think of three reasons why.
3 Explain your reasons.
4 Think of a conclusion.

Useful expressions

I agree/disagree with the statement that …
If we don't ..., we'll …
… instead of … + *-ing* form
I think we should … to …

4 Write your composition.

Paragraph 1: Do you agree or disagree?
Paragraph 2: Give your reasons and explain why.
Paragraph 3: Give your conclusion.

5 Now read your work again. Can you find any errors?

My Portfolio Page 23

My Webpage

Review B

Units 4, 5, 6

1 Complete the words and match them with the pictures.

1 trol*ley – picture 2*
2 shopli _ _ _ _ _
3 hurr _ _ _ _ _
4 debi _ _ _ _ _
5 slo _ _ _
6 dri _ _ _ _ _ _ _ _ _ _ _

2 Write the words in the right category. Add four more words to each one.

Shopping: *trolley, …*
Advertising:
Identity:
Natural disasters:
Crime:

3 In pairs, give definitions for the words in exercise 2. Can your partner guess the correct word?

A *It's a thing you use in a supermarket.*
B *Is it a shopping basket?*
A *No. It's got wheels. …*

THE SHOP

READING – Reality TV

1 Read the advertisement. True or false? Correct the false sentences.

1. *The Shop* is a TV series. *True*
2. In *The Shop*, contestants open a surfing shop.
3. Fifteen Cornwall is a famous nightclub.

Coming soon
The Shop

We are looking for young people to take part in our new reality TV show, *The Shop*. In the series, contestants will open a shop of their choice and compete to run a successful business.

If you take part, you'll have the opportunity to work with top professionals who will help you do market research, design the shop, launch and promote it, and help you run the business.

Your shop will be in the seaside town of Newquay on the north Atlantic coast of Cornwall, in England. Newquay has a population of around 20,000, but this number rises to 100,000 when tourists arrive in the summer.

Over the years, Newquay has become a major tourist destination. It has ten long beaches and the town is known as 'The Surfing Capital of Britain'. It's also famous for its nightlife. Nightclubs such as Sailor's attract international DJs.

Your shop will be close to Watergate Bay, which is famous for its surfing. There's an academy for extreme sports at the bay where you'll also find Fifteen Cornwall, the restaurant that TV chef Jamie Oliver founded to help young people train to become chefs.

You could open a clothes shop, or you might prefer to open a skateboarding, surfing or kite shop. The most important thing is it must be the right shop for Newquay.

During the process, a film crew will follow you 24/7 to record your adventure. If you're interested, you'll have to be quick. Filming will start in three months' time.

2 Complete the sentences. Then write the questions.

1. The shop will be in *Newquay*.
   Where will the shop be?
2. … arrive in Newquay each summer.
3. The town is famous for …
4. … founded Fifteen Cornwall.
5. The most important thing is …
6. Filming will start …

3 Complete the sentences with *that/who*, *that/which*, *where* or nothing.

1. It's the **marketing campaign** *that* makes people aware of the shop.
2. The **shop assistant** is the person … has direct contact with the customer.
3. The **shop window** is … people first see your products.
4. The **design and layout** of the shop are the things … make people buy certain products.

4 In pairs, put the things in exercise 3 in order of importance for a successful shop.

A *I think marketing is most important.*
B *I don't agree. A good shop assistant is more important …*

5 Complete the sentences with *going to*, *will*, *will probably*, *might* or the present continuous. Use each form once.

1. We can confirm that the series *will be* (be) on TV from 5th February next year.
2. Research suggests that it … (be) a big success.
3. We … (have) our auditions on Saturday.
4. We … (audition) as many people as we can.
5. We … (organize) more auditions if we don't find the right people.

LISTENING – Episode one

1 In pairs, speculate about the names of the shops.

Type of shop	Name
computer shop	Checkout
stationer's	The Cure
kite shop	Glacier
chemist's	Laptop
ice-cream shop	Signature
supermarket	Tornado

A *I think the computer shop might be Laptop.*
B *Yes, because a laptop is a type of computer.*

2 Listen to an extract from *The Shop* and answer the questions.

1. Do the contestants like the space?
2. What kind of shop do they want to open?
3. Does the presenter think it's a good idea? Why/Why not?

3 Listen again and choose the correct option.

1. The contestants think the shop isn't too *bad/big*. *bad*
2. The presenter thinks the name *feels/sounds* like the name of a chemist's.
3. They chose the name because it looked cool for the shop's *logo/window*.
4. They*'ve/haven't* done *some/any* market research.
5. The presenter says they'll have to *be original/make money* if they want to win the competition.
6. They think it'll work if they *work hard/ organize a good advertising campaign*.

4 Write complete sentences. Then listen and check.

1. It *isn't as big as* (not / big) we expected.
2. There … (not / enough) space here for all our ideas.
3. It … (not / inspiring) shop space we've seen.
4. We wanted to do something … (original).
5. You can't be … (different).
6. It's the … (important / thing) we've ever done.

SPEAKING

5 In pairs, think of names for these types of shop.

stationer's	ice-cream shop
kite shop	supermarket

A *I think Laptop would be a good name for a computer shop.*
B *Yes. What about the kite shop?*

PROJECT – Open your own shop

1 Think of a shop you'd like to open in Newquay.

clothes shop surf shop kite shop
music shop video games shop

2 Think of a name, and design a logo for your shop.

3 Draw a plan of your shop and name the items.

4 Think of three reasons why your shop is right for Newquay.

5 Present your plan to other students. Choose the best proposal.

SONG Boys don't cry

1 **Can you choose the correct option? Read and check your answers.**

1. Punk rock was … 1970s pop and rock music.
   a influenced by **b** a reaction against
2. Post-punk music was more … than punk.
   a energetic **b** complex
3. The lyrics of a lot of post-punk songs were … .
   a introspective **b** very political

PUNK AND POST-PUNK

Post-punk grew out of the punk rock movement of the mid-1970s. Punk rock, or punk, was a reaction against the commercial pop and rock music of the 1970s. Punk songs were fast, short and simple, and their lyrics were often political or subversive. Post-punk groups like The Cure made music that had punk's energy, but was more complex and experimental, with lyrics that were dark and introspective.

2 **Read and listen to the song. Choose the best summary.**

A His girlfriend left him because he was unkind. He's sad because their relationship has ended, but he isn't showing his real feelings.

B When his girlfriend left him, he wanted to cry. But now he's laughing because he knows that he never really loved her.

I would say I'm sorry
If I thought that it would change your mind
But I know that this time
I have said too much
Been too unkind

Chorus
I try to laugh about it
Cover it all up with lies
I try and laugh about it
Hiding the tears in my eyes
Cause boys don't cry
Boys don't cry

I would break down at your feet
And beg forgiveness
Plead with you
But I know that it's too late
And now there's nothing I can do

Chorus

I would tell you
That I loved you
If I thought that you would stay
But I know that it's no use
That you've already
Gone away

Misjudged your limits
Pushed you too far
Took you for granted
I thought that you needed me more …

Now I would do most anything
To get you back by my side
But I just keep on laughing
Hiding the tears in my eyes
Cause boys don't cry
Boys don't cry
Boys don't cry

3 **How important is a group's image?**

If a group has an original image, …
People notice a group more when …

7 GET PERSONAL

Vocabulary
- Relationships
- Collocations with *have*, *do* and *make*

Grammar
- Second conditional
- *should/shouldn't*
- Second conditional for advice
- First v. second conditional

Speaking
- Do a questionnaire
- Give advice
- Be a mediator

Pronunciation
- *would/ wouldn't*

Writing
- My advice
- *so* and *such*

VOCABULARY – Relationships

1 Put the pictures in order. Then listen and check.

2 Match the sentences with the pictures. Then listen again and check.

1. We *fell in love* quickly. I couldn't stop thinking about her. *picture 3*
2. We *got engaged* and we're *getting married* next month.
3. He started to *chat* me *up* and we *got on* really well.
4. We *fell out* because he told me a lie and we *broke up* for a few weeks.
5. We *went on a date* to the cinema and then we started *going out*.
6. I *got over* it. And he said sorry. So we *made up* and *got back together*.

3 Listen and repeat the expressions.

4 Invent a different story using the pictures.

First they fell in love. Then they got engaged.

My Portfolio Page 24

ARE YOU ROMANTIC?

READING

1 Which of these adjectives would you use to describe yourself? Why?

adventurous independent romantic honest superstitious

I think I'm independent because …

2 Read the questionnaire. Choose a, b or c. Then calculate your score and read the results.

3 Answer the questions.

1 Do you agree with the verdict? Why/why not?
It says I'm not romantic and that's true.
2 Have you ever been on a blind date?
3 What's the most important thing in a relationship?

How romantic are you?

Answer the questions. Then calculate your score to find out how romantic you are.

1 If you met someone on a blind date, he/she would ideally be …
a extremely rich.
b very good-looking.
c someone you could get on with.

2 If you went on a date on Saturday, where would you prefer to go?
a to a dance club
b to a quiet coffee shop
c to the local shopping centre

3 If tomorrow was Valentine's Day, what present would you give your boy/girlfriend?
a concert tickets
b an English dictionary
c six red roses

4 If your boy/girlfriend asked you to get married after going out for a month, you'd say …
a Yes. Let's do it tomorrow.
b What?! You must be joking!
c Let me think about it.

5 You'd break up with your boy/girlfriend if he/she …
a told you lies.
b got a tattoo.
c started smoking.

6 If you broke up with your boy/girlfriend, how long would it take you to get over it?
a probably around six months
b a couple of hours
c I'd never get over it

Score key

1 a–0, b–2, c–4	**4** a–4, b–0, c–2
2 a–2, b–4, c–0	**5** a–4, b–0, c–2
3 a–2, b–0, c–4	**6** a–2, b–0, c–4

The Verdict

0–6	You're not very romantic. If you don't add some romance to your life, you might never meet the girl or boy of your dreams!
8–16	OK, you're quite romantic, but don't only think about yourself. There are two people in a relationship.
18–24	Are you too romantic? Maybe you expect too much from the person you fall in love with.

GRAMMAR Second conditional

*You'**d break up** with your boyfriend **if** he **told** you lies.*
***If** your girlfriend **asked** you to get married, you'**d say** yes.*
***If** you **went** on a date on Saturday, where **would** you **prefer** to go?*

	Hypothetical situation	Result
If	+ past simple	+ would / wouldn't + infinitive
If	she **asked** you, you **went** on a date,	you'**d say** 'yes'. where **would** you **go**?

1 Write the verbs in the correct form.

1 If I *met* (meet) someone special, I*'d ask* (ask) them to go on a date.
2 If someone special … (ask) me to go on a date, I … (say) OK!
3 We … (start) the evening at the cinema if we … (have) enough money.
4 If we … (not have) enough money, we … (go) for a walk.
5 We … (not go) for a walk if it … (be) very cold.
6 If the weather … (be) bad, we … (stay) at home.

2 Complete the dialogue. Then listen and check.

Jo What (1) *would you do* (you /do) if your boyfriend went on a date with another girl?
Lorna If he went on a date with another girl, I (2) … (ask) him to explain why.
Jo And if (3) … (he / not / explain), would you break up with him?
Lorna Yes, I (4) … .
Jo And if he said he was sorry, (5) … (you / get back together)?
Lorna No, I (6) … . If (7) … (he / go out) with another girl, (8) … (I / not / go out) with him again.
Jo Good.
Lorna What do you mean 'good'?
Jo Nothing. It's just a hypothetical situation.

Pronunciation

would/wouldn't

3 Listen and repeat the sentences from exercise 2.

4 Write the questions. Then answer them.

1 What / you / do / if / you / find / 50 euros on the street ?
What would you do if you found 50 euros on the street? I'd take it to the police station.
2 If / you / see / a robbery / what / you / do ?
3 What / you / say / if / your best friend / tell / you / a lie ?
4 If / a friend / organize / a blind date / you / go ?
5 you / agree / if / a TV company / ask / you / to dance / in public ?
6 What / you / do / if / you / break / a neighbour's window ?

GO 4 IT!

5 Choose one of the questionnaire titles and prepare four questions.

How adventurous are you?
How superstitious are you?
How honest are you?

If you won a free holiday, would you go:
a on safari in Africa?
b to a hotel on Ibiza?
c on a cruise around the Mediterranean?

6 Ask a partner your questions. What's the verdict?

A *If you won a free holiday, would you go …?*
B *I'd go on a safari.*
A *The verdict is – you're very adventurous.*

HELP!

VOCABULARY Collocations with *have*, *do* and *make*

1 Find the people in the picture.

1–B

1 He's having a party.
2 They're making fun of her.
3 They're having an argument.
4 She's doing something wrong.

2 Copy and complete the diagrams. Listen and check. Then listen and repeat.

a mistake	a conversation	nothing
~~an effort~~	a good time	an excuse

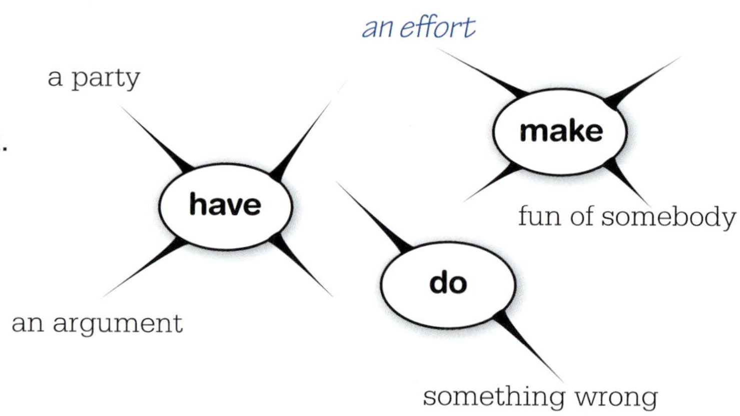

LISTENING

3 Listen to a radio show. Two teenagers, Shayla and Ben, phone and ask Sue for advice. Can you find them in the picture above?

4 Listen again. Choose the correct option.

1 – a

1 Shayla's relationship with her boyfriend is good when …
a they're on their own. **b** his friends are around.
2 Sue thinks he …
a understands how she feels. **b** feels embarrassed.
3 She thinks Shayla should find another boyfriend if …
a he won't speak to her. **b** he doesn't act differently.
4 Ben made a mistake when he …
a put the invitation on the Internet. **b** went on holiday for a week.
5 During the party, …
a people broke a lot of things. **b** his parents came back.
6 Sue thinks he should …
a ask his parents to forgive him. **b** pay for the damage.

5 Do you agree with Sue? What would you do?

I think Shayla's problem is normal. I think she should be patient.

GRAMMAR

should/shouldn't

*You **should talk** to him about it. You **shouldn't lie**.*

1 Give advice for the problems.

1. I get very stressed.
   I think you should do yoga.
2. I want to have a party.
3. I'd like to be famous.
4. I had an argument with one of my friends.
5. I'd like to buy some clothes but I haven't got much money.
6. I haven't done my homework.

Second conditional for advice

*If I **were** you, I'**d have** a conversation with him.*
*I'**d promise** to pay if I **were** you.*

2 Write the sentences. Then match them with a problem in exercise 1. Is it the same as your advice?

1. If I / be / you I / not make / an excuse
   If I were you, I wouldn't make an excuse. – 6
2. I / learn / to sing / if I / be / you
3. If I / be / you I / not put / it on the Internet
4. I / not worry / about it if I / be / you
5. If I / be / you I / not spend / all my time studying
6. If I / be / you I / go / to a market

First v. second conditional

*If you **pay**, your parents **will** forgive you.*
*If I **were** you, I'**d** promise to pay.*

First conditional possible situation	If + present, will/won't + infinitive If you pay, your parents will forgive you.
Second conditional hypothetical situation	If + past, would/wouldn't + infinitive If I were you, I'd promise to pay.

3 Choose the correct option.

1. I*'ll do* / *'d do* the washing-up if you help me with my homework. *'ll do*
2. If my brother *isn't* / *wasn't* lazy, he wouldn't get into trouble.
3. If you didn't stay up late, you *won't feel* / *wouldn't feel* tired in the morning.
4. Our teacher will be angry if we *arrive* / *arrived* late again.
5. We *won't go* / *wouldn't* go to the park if it's cold on Saturday.
6. We*'ll travel* / *'d travel* around the world if we won the lottery.

4 Complete the dialogue. Then listen and check.

Tim Hi, Sue. My problem is that my girlfriend wants me to spend all my time with her.
Sue Well, if you don't see your friends, you (1) *'ll lose* (lose) them. If I were you, I (2) … (go out) together in a group.
Tim But we often talk about sport, and she gets bored.
Sue Well, if I (3) … (be) her, I'd feel the same. Why don't you invite her friends? If she (4) … (have) other people to talk to, she won't get bored. And I (5) … (not talk) about sport all the time if I were you. If you do, I think she (6) … (find) another boyfriend.

GO 4 IT!

5 Invent a problem. Use the ideas to help you.

You did something wrong at school.
You had an argument with someone.
You want to be healthier.

6 In pairs, explain the problem and give advice. Then choose the best advice.

A *I got bad results at school. Now I'm grounded.*
B *If I were you, I'd … If you … your parents won't …*

Culture

SCHOOL MEDIATORS

1 Answer the questions.

1 How common are the problems below at your school?
Stealing's not very common. Nobody's stolen anything from me.

stealing vandalism graffiti
disputes between students

2 What action does the school take?

2 Rashid's a school mediator. What does he do? Read the first paragraph and check.

a He creates conflicts.
b He helps to resolve conflicts.

3 Read again. Match the questions below with Rashid's answers.

a – 3

a What happens next?
b What does a mediator do?
c How did you become a mediator?
d Do you think you're a good mediator?
e Why do you think peer mediation has worked so well?

4 True or false? Correct the false sentences.

1 Rashid's school doesn't have any conflicts.
False – His school is difficult.
2 Only students with good reputations can be mediators.
3 You have to train to be a mediator.
4 Rashid doesn't tell anybody else the things he hears during mediation.
5 He chooses the best solution for the conflict.
6 Mediation helps students to understand how other people feel.

Quest

- Which rock group recorded a song called 'Mediate'?

Rashid is fifteen. He describes his school as difficult, but smiles when he tells me that things are getting better. The school uses mediation to resolve conflicts like vandalism, stealing and disputes between pupils. I met Rashid to find out how it works.

1 …

The school was looking for volunteers, and I said I was interested. They thought I was joking because I had a bad reputation. But they saw I was serious, and let me do the training.

2 …

The people in a conflict see things differently. So the first thing we do is listen to both sides. I guarantee that anything they tell me will be confidential. And because I'm another student, they talk to me.

3 …

We get the two sides to talk. First, they have to listen to the other side without interrupting. That's important. Then they talk about possible solutions, and agree on the best solution for everybody.

4 …

Because it makes people stop and think. Some boys here were vandalizing the toilets – breaking things, making a mess, writing graffiti. During mediation, they met the cleaner, and they saw how their actions affected another person. If you punish people, they feel bad. But if you get people to listen to each other, they learn something. They feel respected.

5 …

Yeah, I think so. I always used to be in trouble, so I think I understand the conflicts better than someone who's never done anything bad.

ENGLISH YOU NEED – Be a mediator

1 Listen and match the dialogue with one of the pictures.

①

②

③

2 Listen again and answer the questions.

1 What was Emma watching? *A soap opera*
2 What did John do?
3 What does John want to watch? Why?
4 What solution does Tim suggest?

3 Listen and complete what Tim says.

1 Hey! What's *going on*?
2 Emma, what … …?
3 Is … …, John?
4 Emma, … him finish.
5 You changed channel. That isn't … .
6 I've got an idea. … … you record the music programme?
7 That …, you can both see what you want.
8 Does that … fair, Emma?

4 Listen and repeat.

5 Complete the dialogue with words or phrases from exercise 3.

Jo (1) *What's going* on?
Mark We were playing here first!
Olga You didn't let us play!
Jo (2) Olga, … exactly?
Olga We were waiting for about twenty minutes, and they didn't let us play.
Jo (3) …, Mark?
Mark Yes.
Jo (4) … fair. The net's for everyone.
Mark But there's only one.
Jo Why don't you play in two teams? (5) … way, you can all play.
Mark OK.
Jo Does (6) …, Olga?
Olga Yes.

6 In pairs, prepare and practise a similar dialogue for the situation in picture 2, or for a different situation.

WRITING – My advice

1 If your boy or girlfriend got a piercing in his/her lip, what would you do?

2 Read the website posting and the two replies. Who gives the best advice?

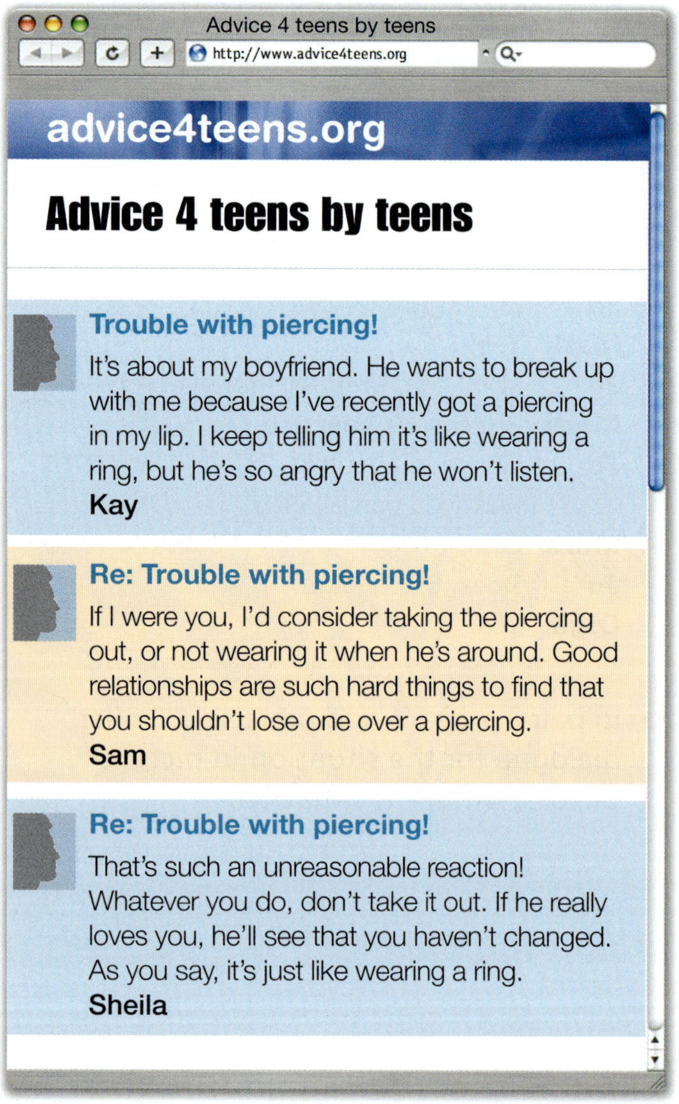

Advice 4 teens by teens

http://www.advice4teens.org

advice4teens.org

Advice 4 teens by teens

Trouble with piercing!

It's about my boyfriend. He wants to break up with me because I've recently got a piercing in my lip. I keep telling him it's like wearing a ring, but he's so angry that he won't listen.

Kay

Re: Trouble with piercing!

If I were you, I'd consider taking the piercing out, or not wearing it when he's around. Good relationships are such hard things to find that you shouldn't lose one over a piercing.

Sam

Re: Trouble with piercing!

That's such an unreasonable reaction! Whatever you do, don't take it out. If he really loves you, he'll see that you haven't changed. As you say, it's just like wearing a ring.

Sheila

so and *such*

*He's **so** angry **that** he won't listen.*
*That's **such an unreasonable** reaction!*
*Good relationships are **such hard things** to find **that** …*

3 Complete the rules.

1. … + adjective
2. … a(n) + adjective + singular noun
3. … + adjective + plural noun

4 Complete the sentences *so* or *such*.

1. I have to be home *so* early that I can never go to concerts.
2. I've got … a strict mum that I can't do anything.
3. My boyfriend gets … jealous that he stops me speaking to other boys.
4. My friend makes … long calls that he uses all my credit!
5. I can't go on holiday with friends because my parents are … worried about it.
6. I can't buy my girlfriend an MP3 player for her birthday because it's … an expensive present.

Useful expressions

It's about …
I keep telling him … but he won't listen.
I'd consider … *-ing* form …
Whatever you do, don't …
As you say, …

5 Makes notes. Then write replies with advice for two of the problems in exercise 4.

6 Now read your work again. Can you find any errors?

My Portfolio Page 25

My Webpage

8 WONDERS

Vocabulary
- Monuments
- Mysteries

Grammar
- Passive: present and past
- Passive: questions

Speaking
- Choose your favourite buildings
- An interview about a mystery
- Express doubt

Pronunciation
- Intonation

Writing
- My choice
- Linkers of reason

VOCABULARY Monuments

1 Match the words with the pictures. Listen and check. Then listen and repeat.

1 – wall

pyramid | church | ~~wall~~ | monastery | opera house
lighthouse | mosque | skyscraper | temple | palace

1 The Great Wall

2 The Parthenon

3 Versailles

4 Chichen Itza

5 The Empire State Building

6 La Scala

7 St Mark's Basilica

8 The Sultan Ahmed

9 Taktshang

10 The Pharos

2 Match the monuments with the countries.

1 – The Great Wall – China

Egypt Italy France ~~China~~ Bhutan
Greece Turkey the USA Italy Mexico

3 Can you complete the list with monuments in the pictures?

The New Seven Wonders of the World 2007

1 The Taj Mahal, India
2 Christ Redeemer, Brazil
3 Colosseum, Italy
4 Machu Picchu, Peru
5 Petra, Jordan
6 …
7 …

My Portfolio Page 26

MY SEVEN WONDERS

READING

1 Which place do you think …?

a contains plants from all over the world
The Eden Project
b opened in 2000
c is over 100 years old
d was very unpopular with local people

2 Read and check your answers.

In 2007, the new Seven Wonders of the world were announced. They included the Colosseum in Rome and the Great Wall of China. So I decided to start a list of my own seven wonders. Here's the list so far!

1 The London Eye
It was built for the new millennium, but it wasn't opened until March 2000. Typical! It's 135 metres high and there are 32 capsules. It takes half an hour to go round and it never stops so you have to get on and off while it's moving.

2 The Angel of the North
A lot of people hated this statue when it was first built in 1998, but now it's a popular icon. It's made of steel and stands near the road to Newcastle. It's twenty metres high and the wings are 54 metres wide, that's wider than a Boeing 757.

3 The Eden Project
It looks like something from space, but you can see plants from all over the world here. The domes were built to create different climates, so you can see banana trees in the tropical dome and olive trees and grape vines in the Mediterranean one.

4 Blackpool Tower
It was built after the mayor of Blackpool visited Paris and saw the Eiffel Tower. The first stone was laid in 1891 and there's a time capsule buried under it. You can take a lift to the top, and there's also an aquarium and a circus at the base.

3 Read again. Choose the correct answer.

1 The London Eye opened *on time* / *late* for the new millennium. *late*
2 It *stops* / *doesn't stop* for people to get on or off.
3 The Angel of the North is *higher* / *wider* than an aeroplane.
4 The Eden Project is an educational *space* / *nature* project.
5 Blackpool Tower has a time capsule *at the top of* / *under* it.
6 There are fun things to do *near* / *at the bottom of* the tower.

4 Answer the questions.

1 Which place would you prefer to visit? Why?
2 Are there any buildings in your country that local people don't like?

GRAMMAR Passive: present and past

It's made of steel. It wasn't opened until March 2000.

	Affirmative	Negative
Present	It's made of steel.	It isn't used for anything.
Past	It was built for the millennium.	It wasn't opened until 2000.

1 Write the verbs in the present passive.

not make collect control
give not import ~~locate~~

1 The Eden Project*'s located* in the south-west of England.
2 The domes … of glass, but of a special type of plastic.
3 Temperatures inside the domes … by a computer.
4 Rainwater … to water the plants.
5 The food in the restaurants is grown locally, it … .
6 People who arrive on foot or by bicycle … a discount on the entry price.

2 Write the verbs in the past passive.

1 Different parts *were constructed* (construct) between the 6th century BC and the 16th century AD.
2 It …(design) by Heitor da Silva Costa.
3 The buildings … (cut) into the mountains.
4 Individual sections … (not connect) until the Qin Dynasty in 221–206 BC.
5 It … (not discover) until 1812, when a Swiss explorer found it.
6 It … (build) between 1922 and 1931.

3 Decide which places the sentences describe.

Christ Redeemer Petra
The Great Wall of China

4 Write the verbs in the present or past passive. Then listen and check.

The Taj Mahal (**1**) *was built* (build) for Emperor Shah Jahan to honour the memory of his favourite wife.
It (**2**) … (make) out of white marble, and it (**3**) … (set) in a 300-square-metre garden. Over 22,000 workers and 1,000 elephants (**4**) … (involve) in the construction of the building, which (**5**) … (complete) in about 1648. Later, people say that the emperor (**6**) … (put) in prison, and he could only see it from the window of his prison cell.

5 Active or passive? Choose the correct option.

1 Machu Picchu *built / was built* by Emperor Pachacutec in about 1450. *was built*
2 The people *abandoned / were abandoned* it later because of disease.
3 It *didn't rediscover / wasn't rediscovered* until 1911.
4 Hiram Bingham, an American historian, *found / was found* it.
5 Unfortunately, he *didn't leave / wasn't left* the site untouched.
6 He took some things back to the USA, where they *keep / are kept* in a museum.

GO 4 IT!

6 Make a list of four wonders in your country. Use these ideas to help you.

cathedral theme park stadium
statue skyscraper

7 Make notes about the places. Then tell a partner. Agree on the top four places.

date (approximately)
location why you like it

I like the Nou Camp Stadium. It's in …

MYSTERIOUS WORLD

VOCABULARY – Mysteries

1 Complete the sentences. Then listen and check.

case | clues | evidence
fact | ~~mystery~~ | theories

1 Nobody knows why the passengers and crew of the Mary Celeste disappeared. It's a *mystery.*
2 We know that the ship was found abandoned on 4th December 1872. That's a …
3 People have different ideas about what happened. These are just …
4 Some people believe there was a tsunami. There's no … of this.
5 People have explored the ship looking for signs of what happened. There aren't enough …
6 We will probably never know what happened. The … is still open.

2 Listen and repeat the phrases.

LISTENING

3 Listen to the radio programme and answer the questions.

1 Which of the mysteries do they talk about?
a Easter island **b** The Bermuda Triangle
c The Nazca lines
2 What pictures do they look at?
a satellite pictures **b** ancient drawings
c Dr Bach's photo album

Easter island

Nazca lines

4 True or false? Correct the false sentences.

1 The lines are in the Atacama Desert in Peru. *True*
2 They are about 3,000 years old.
3 There are many different types of lines.
4 You can see them very well from ground level.
5 One theory is that the lines had a religious significance.
6 Experts now know that aliens used the lines to help them land their spaceships.

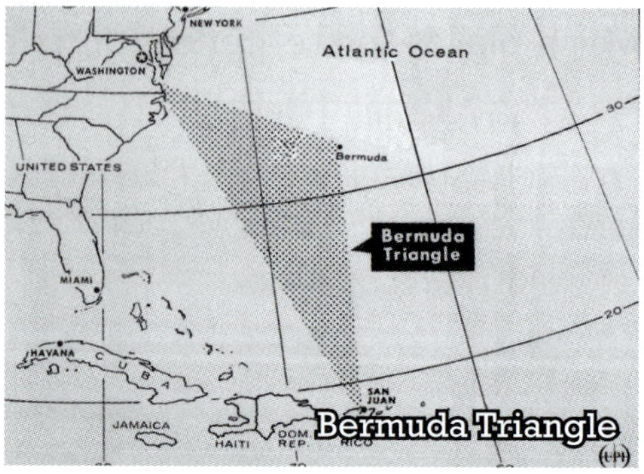

Bermuda Triangle

GRAMMAR Passive: questions

*Where **are** these lines **located**?*
***Were** they **used** by aliens?*

Question word	*be*	Subject	Past participle	Agent
Where	are	these lines	located?	
	Were	they	used	by aliens?

1 Write the questions. Then match them with the answers.

1 where / Easter Island / locate ?
Where is Easter Island located? – c
2 what languages / speak / there ?
3 who / the island / own / by ?
4 when / the statues / make ?
5 why / they / put there ?
6 when / the island first / discover / by Europeans ?

a It's part of Chile.
b On 5th April 1772. A Dutch explorer found it.
c In the Pacific Ocean.
d Between 400 and 1700.
e Spanish and Rapa Nui.
f Nobody knows, but perhaps they represented ancestors.

2 Write the questions. Then listen and check.

Hilary Have you heard about the Marree Man?
Jeff No. When (1) *was he discovered* (he / discover) ?
Hilary In 1998. Look, here's a picture.
Jeff That's amazing! How (2) … (he / find) ?
Hilary A pilot first saw him.
Jeff Where (3) … (he / locate) ?
Hilary In southern Australia.
Jeff How (4) … (the lines / make) ?
Hilary By a tractor, apparently.
Jeff And who (5) … (he / create) by?
Hilary Nobody knows!
Jeff That's fascinating.

Intonation

3 Listen to the phrases. Which show interest, the first ones or the second ones?

4 Listen and repeat. Show interest.

5 Write active or passive questions for the underlined information.

1 The Bermuda Triangle is located in the Atlantic Ocean.
Where is the Bermuda Triangle located?
2 People first heard about lights in the sky in this area in 1492.
3 The lights were reported by Christopher Columbus.
4 The Bermuda Triangle is important because ships and planes have disappeared here.
5 Some people think there's a supernatural explanation.
6 The idea was used by Stephen Spielberg in the film *Close Encounters*.

GO 4 IT!

6 Choose one of the mysteries from this page, or another mystery. In pairs, prepare and practise a radio interview about your mystery. (You can invent!)

A *Welcome to 'Beyond the Third Dimension'. Today we are joined by Dr Esteban …*
B *Good afternoon.*
A *Dr Esteban. Where's the … located?*

Culture

THE FIRST EMPEROR

1 Look at the photo. Can you answer these questions?

1. What can you see in the photo?
2. Where are they from?
3. How old are they?
   a about 500 years b about 1,000 years c more than 2,000 years
4. How big are they?
   a smaller than real people b life-sized c bigger than real people

2 Read and check your answers.

Qin Museum

Opening Hours: 08.00 to 18.00
Duration of a visit: 3 hours
Admission Fee: CNY 90

Visitors to the museum can see Emperor Qin Shi Huang's famous Terracotta Army. The discovery of these life-sized warriors and horses in Xian in 1974 was the most important archaeological find of the 20th century. The area was declared a World Heritage site by UNESCO in 1987.

The statues were buried when Qin Shi Huang died in 210 BC, but work started on his tomb when he came to power in 246 BC, at the age of thirteen. Qin Shi Huang was China's first Emperor; he was the man who created China from states that were at war for two centuries. He also built one of China's Great Walls. He was undoubtedly one of history's greatest leaders.

Although the location of Qin Shi Huang's 80-metre-high tomb was well-known, his Terracotta Army was discovered by accident. The first statue was found one-and-a-half kilometres from the tomb by local workmen. Since then, archaeologists have uncovered thousands of statues, and work continues at the site. The army guards an enormous underground palace.

The tomb itself remains closed. Ancient documents say that there are rivers of mercury in it, and that it is protected against intruders, so archaeologists are not sure whether to open the tomb now or wait until they have a better idea of what's inside.

3 Answer the questions.

1. When was the Terracotta Army discovered? *It was discovered in 1974.*
2. When were the statues buried?
3. Where was the first statue found?
4. Who found it?
5. How do archeologists know what might be in the tomb?
6. When are they going to open the tomb?

4 Complete the sentences about Qin Shi Huang.

1. He came to power when he was *thirteen*.
2. He died when he was ... .
3. He is very important in Chinese history because ... .
4. Apart from his tomb, he built ... .

Quest

- Find three World Heritage sites in your country. What can you see at the sites?

ENGLISH YOU NEED Express doubt

1 Listen to the dialogues between Marie and Bernard. What's the connection between the dialogues?

a Marie needs to make a decision.
b Marie has doubts about something.
c Marie doesn't believe Bernard.

2 Listen again and complete the extracts.

Dialogue 1

Marie Do you think they'll open Emperor Qin's tomb?
Bernard I (1) *don't know.* They think it's got mercury in it.
Marie I'm not (2) … … that's true. It's 2,000 years old. I (3) … … they knew about mercury then.

Dialogue 2

Bernard Are you going to the U2 concert next month?
Marie I (4) … … .
Bernard Why? You love U2.
Marie The tickets are really expensive. And their last album was terrible.
Bernard Do you (5) … … so?
Marie Yes. I like the older songs, and I'm not (6) … … they'll play them. Are you going to go?
Bernard I'm not (7) … . I'll go if you go, but I don't (8) … … I want to go alone.

3 Listen and repeat.

4 Order the words and write the phrases in the dialogue.

1 not / I'm / convinced / that
2 doubt / it / I
3 doubt / I / if / could / I
4 know / my marks / don't / I / if
5 if / sure / not / that's true / I'm
6 so / think / you / do / really

Marie Your dad's a doctor. Do you think you'll study medicine?
Bernard (1) *I doubt it.* (2) … will be good enough.
Marie (3) … . You did well in your last exams.
Bernard But (4) … I'd be a good doctor.
Marie You'd be a great doctor!
Bernard (5) …? They have to work really long hours. (6) … do that. I'm too lazy.

5 In pairs, prepare and practise a dialogue for one of these questions.

1 Do you think they'll find life on Mars?
2 Are you going to go to a music festival this summer?
3 Do you think aliens have visited our planet?
4 Are you going to get a tattoo?

WRITING – My choice

1 What are the connections between the picture and things in the box?

3,500 – It could be how old the monument is.

~~3,500~~ Stonehenge 380 kilometres
religious ceremonies 40 tonnes

2 Read the Internet posting and check your answers to exercise 1.

My candidate for the top British wonder is Stonehenge. It's 3,500 years old and it's Britain's most important prehistoric monument.

I've chosen Stonehenge because of the mystery that surrounds it. Some people believe it was built for religious ceremonies. Others think it was an astronomical observatory. Nobody knows for sure. That's why it's fascinating to visit and learn about it.

I also think Stonehenge is special because it was so difficult to build. Some stones weigh forty tonnes but were brought from 380 kilometres away.

For all these reasons I think Stonehenge should be our top British Wonder.

Roland

Linkers of reason

*I've also chosen it **because of** the mystery that surrounds it.*
***That's why** it's fascinating to visit it.*
*Stonehenge is special **because** it was so difficult to build.*

It's interesting **because** it's mysterious. = It's mysterious. **That's why** it's interesting.
It's my top choice **because of** the mystery that surrounds it. = It's mysterious. **That's why** it's my top choice.

3 Write *because*, *because of* or *that's why* in the descriptions.

My candidate is the monastery of Wearmouth-Jarrow. I haven't chosen it **(1)** *because* it's beautiful, but **(2)** … its importance. It was one of the world's greatest centres of learning. **(3)** … I think it should be our British Wonder.

Frank

The Palace of Westminster should be our British Wonder. It's my choice **(4)** … its location in the centre of London, and **(5)** … this is where our parliament makes its laws. But it's also an architectural masterpiece, and **(6)** … it's my top candidate.

Patricia

Useful expressions

My candidate for … is …
Some people believe …
Others think …
Nobody knows for sure.
For all these reasons I think …

4 Make notes. Then write about your candidate for the wonder of your country.

Paragraph 1: Your first reason for choosing it.
Paragraph 2: Another reason for choosing it.
Paragraph 3: Your final reason for choosing it.
Paragraph 4: Your conclusion.

5 Now read your work again. Can you find any errors?

My Portfolio Page 27

My Webpage

9 THE FRONT PAGE

Vocabulary
- Newspapers
- Reporting verbs

Grammar
- Past perfect
- Past perfect: questions
- Reported speech
- *say* and *tell*

Speaking
- Invent a news story
- Hold a press conference
- Gossip

Pronunciation
- Vowel sound: /ɜː/

Writing
- A news article
- Time connectors

VOCABULARY – Newspapers

1 Match the words with the newspaper. Listen and check. Then listen and repeat.

1 – front page

caption | cartoon | ~~front page~~ | headline | horoscope
local news | sports section | world news | weather forecast

2 Answer the questions.

1. Do you ever read a newspaper?
   I sometimes read a free newspaper when I'm on the bus.
2. If so, what newspapers do you read? What part of a newspaper do you read first? What other parts do you read?
3. If not, why not?

My Portfolio Page 28

IN THE NEWS

READING

1 Look at the headlines. Then answer the questions.

① **Boy travels 2,000 kilometres to keep holiday romance alive**

② **Trainers save boy's life in lightning strike**

1 Who did the boy go to see? Why?
Maybe he went to see his girlfriend.
2 What do you think happened?
3 Where do you think the boy was?
4 What do you think he was doing?

2 Read the stories. Were your ideas correct?

①

An Italian boy hitchhiked 2,000 kilometres to see a girl in Sweden. The fifteen-year-old had met the girl on holiday, but couldn't stop thinking about her when he got back to Milan.

Enzo Rossi was stopped by police at a motorway service station near Stockholm because his parents had reported him as missing. They were worried because he hadn't told them about his plans.

When they heard his story, the police contacted the girl's parents. They agreed that the youngsters could meet. But when the girl's father arrived, he drove the boy straight to the airport. His daughter had decided that she didn't want to see the boy again.

②

A boy was saved by his trainers when lightning struck his house. The boy was speaking on the phone when a huge shock made him scream with pain and drop the handset.

The fifteen-year-old boy was talking to his girlfriend about the presents they had received on Christmas Day when the lightning struck. He heard a crash of thunder, felt a shock up his arm and then the lights went out. He later found out that the rubber soles of his trainers had saved his life. He had only had them for 24 hours.

Alex's mother, a single parent, had saved for a long time to buy the trainers, but said that they were the best thing she had ever bought.

3 Read the two news stories and correct the sentences.

Story 1

1 His parents knew he was going to Stockholm. *They didn't know about his plans.*
2 The police stopped him in Stockholm.
3 He hitchhiked back to Milan.

Story 2

4 The lightning didn't hurt the boy.
5 He phoned his girlfriend on Christmas Day.
6 His trainers were a Christmas present from his girlfriend.

GRAMMAR

Past perfect

The boy was stopped because his parents ***had reported*** *him as missing.*
They were worried because he ***hadn't told*** *them his plans.*

	Subject	*had(n't)*	Past participle
Affirmative	They	'd	reported him as missing.
Negative	He	hadn't	told them about his plans.

1 Write the past perfect of the verbs.

fall forget give meet not hear ~~not see~~

1 Luigi went to the USA to visit relatives that he *hadn't seen* before.
2 He spent a lot of time there with a girl he … on the plane.
3 When he returned home, he realized that he … in love with her.
4 He couldn't phone her because he … her phone number.
5 He felt sad because he … from her since the holiday.
6 Then he remembered that she … him her address.

2 Write sentences with the past perfect.

1 The film started. We arrived at the cinema. (when)
The film had started when we arrived at the cinema.
2 My mum was unhappy. I didn't buy her a present. (because)
3 The train left. She got to the station. (when)
4 I got up late. My alarm clock stopped. (because)
5 We couldn't go to the concert. We didn't reserve tickets. (because)
6 I didn't finish my exam. The bell rang. (when)

Past perfect: questions

Had *he* ***met*** *her before?* *Where* ***had*** *they* ***met****?*

Question word	*had*	Subject	Past participle
	Had	he	met her before?
Where	had	they	met?
Short answers	Yes, he had.		No, he hadn't.

3 Complete an interview with Enzo's father. Then listen and check.

Jane (1) *Had Enzo been* (Enzo / be) to Sweden before?
Aldo No, he (2) … . It was the first time.
Jane How often (3) … (they / be) in contact before he set off?
Aldo He (4) … (not hear) a word from her.
Jane (5) … (he / write) to her?
Aldo Yes, he (6) …, but she'd returned his letter. That really hurt his feelings!

Pronunciation

Vowel sound: /ɜː/

4 Listen and repeat the words.

first heard word her returned hurt

5 Listen and repeat the sentences.

GO 4 IT!

6 In pairs, choose a headline. Write a short news story. Then tell the story to another pair.

Dog saves boy Girl finds fortune Teenager stops bank robbery

On Saturday night, a dog saved a teenager who had fallen into a river.

PRESS CONFERENCE

VOCABULARY Reporting verbs

1 Match the verbs with the comments. Listen and check. Then listen and repeat.

admit (v) – confess that something is true
claim (v) – say something is a fact
confirm (v) – say that a rumour or belief is correct
insist (v) – repeat something for emphasis
reveal (v) – say something that has been a secret
deny (v) – say that something isn't true

1 Yes, what you think is correct. *confirm*
2 I've said this before and I'll say it again, ...
3 OK, it's true.

4 I haven't told anyone before, but ...
5 That's not true!
6 It's a fact. I'm the best director.

LISTENING

2 Listen to the press conference with Olivier Ford, film director, and Sharon Diamond, actress. Which things do they talk about?

1 – reviews of Olivier's new film

~~reviews of Olivier's new film~~
Olivier and Sharon's working relationship
Olivier's personal life
Sharon's personal life   their next film

3 Read the article written after the press conference. Can you find six differences? Listen again to check.

1 – She didn't confirm rumours that she had argued with Olivier.

Sharon and Olivier talk about *The Truth*

At yesterday's press conference, Olivier Ford said he wasn't worried about what the critics said about his new film. He claimed that he made films for the ordinary person on the street.

Sharon Diamond finally confirmed rumours that she had argued with Olivier during the making of the film. She insisted that she hadn't enjoyed working with him at all.

When she was asked about her husband, she said that she'd seen him but they hadn't talked. She also admitted that she was going out with the young star, Sean Willis.

Olivier denied that he was going to work with Sharon again. He revealed that his new film would be similar to his last film. He also told reporters that the film would star Sean Willis.

GRAMMAR

Reported speech

*He said he **wasn't** worried. She said that she**'d seen** him.*

Direct speech		Reported speech
Present simple 'I'**m not** worried.'	→	Past simple He said (that) he **wasn't** worried.
Present continuous 'I'**m not going out** with Sean.'	→	Past continuous She said (that) she **wasn't going out** with Sean.
Present perfect 'I'**ve seen** him.'	→	Past perfect She said (that) she **had seen** him.
Past simple 'We **didn't argue**.'	→	Past perfect She said (that) they **hadn't argued**.
will + infinitive 'My next film **will be** different.'	→	*would* + infinitive He said (that) his next film **would be** different.

1 Write what the critic said.

1 'I didn't enjoy the film at all.'
He said he hadn't enjoyed the film at all.
2 'Olivier isn't getting on well with his actors.'
3 'Olivier hasn't made a good film for years.'
4 'Sharon didn't perform well in her role.'
5 'I'm very disappointed.'
6 'I won't go to see Olivier's next film.'

say and *tell*

say	He said (that) he wasn't worried.
tell + object	He told **us** (that) he wasn't worried.

2 Write *said* or *told*.

1 Olivier *told* us he didn't read reviews.
2 He ... he never had problems with actors.
3 He ... me his next film would be a drama.
4 Sharon ... us that Olivier had been fantastic.
5 She also ... that she didn't want to talk about her personal life.
6 She ... she was concentrating on her career.

3 Write in reported speech. Use reporting verbs.

admit claim confirm ~~deny~~ insist reveal

1 'That's not true. I didn't take the money.'
2 'Our party will win the next election.'
3 'Yes, the band is going on tour.'
4 'We haven't told anyone yet, but we got married in June.'
5 'I've said it before, and I'll say it again. I don't make commercial films.'
6 'OK, it's true. I've signed for Manchester United.'

1 The thief ...
The thief denied that he had taken the money.
2 The president ...
3 The lead singer ...
4 The couple ...
5 The director ...
6 Ronald ...

GO 4 IT!

4 In pairs, prepare a press conference. Prepare questions to ask a group of musicians.

What's the name of your new album?

5 Ask another pair your questions. Then answer their questions. (You can invent!)

A *What's the name of your new album?*
B *We don't have a name yet.*

6 Write a short article about the interview.

At yesterday's press conference, Bob and Shirin revealed that their group didn't have a name ...

Culture

WHY GOSSIP?

1 Answer the questions.

1 Do you know the names of any 'gossip' magazines?
I know 'Hello' but I don't know any others.
2 Do you ever read them? Which ones?
3 Which celebrities are in the news at the moment? Why?

2 Which sentence do you think is true? Read the article to check your answers.

1 Most people enjoy gossiping.
2 Gossiping is the same as grooming for animals.
3 Some celebrities like appearing in gossip columns.

We talk to other people in a lot of different ways. We tell jokes and stories, explain things and share secrets. But the thing we enjoy doing most is gossiping.

Have you heard ...?

by Lucy Strong

Its true! We all enjoy talking about other people, or listening to people talk about other people, especially if those people are friends or celebrities. I know I do.

According to some scientists, gossiping is a natural part of living together in groups. Other primates, such as baboons, use grooming to establish social connections. Human groups have become too large for grooming and so we gossip instead.

Unfortunately, while gossiping is an excellent way to share facts and opinions, it's also an easy way to give false information. There are a lot of magazines that are full of gossip about rich and famous people. Many newspapers have 'gossip columns' in which journalists write about the social and personal lives of celebrities.

But how much of this gossip is true? Many celebrities deliberately create gossip to stay in the news. The Irish poet, Oscar Wilde, once said, 'There is only one thing in the world worse than being talked about, and that is not being talked about.'

And don't forget the Spanish proverb. It tells us not to listen to someone who gossips to us. Sooner or later, they'll gossip about us to someone else.

By the way, did you hear what happened to our editor last week? Well, I heard ...

Baboons grooming. Taking dirt and parasites from another animal's fur has an important social function.

Gossiping is a natural part of living together in groups.

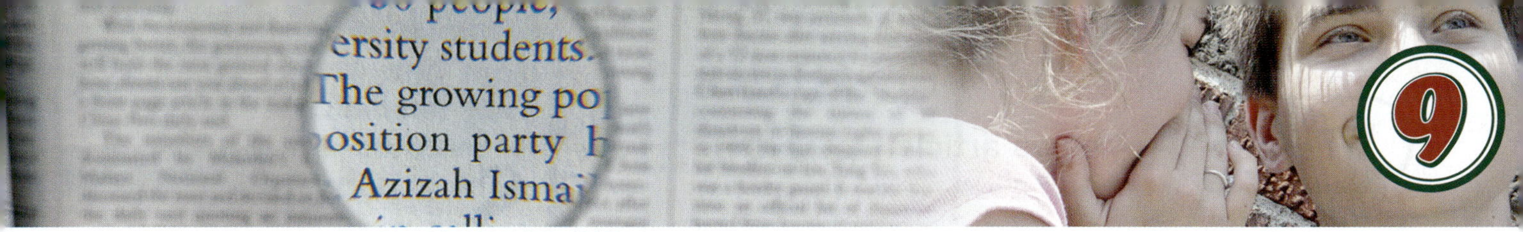

3 Read again and answer the questions.

1 What are some different ways that people talk to each other?
We tell jokes and stories, explain things and share secrets.
2 Why do baboons groom each other?
3 Why don't human beings groom?
4 What's a good thing about gossiping?
5 Why is it sometimes bad?
6 Why do some celebrities create gossip?

4 How do you say Oscar Wilde's saying and the proverb in your language?

Quest

- Find another quote or proverb in English. Translate it into your language.

ENGLISH YOU NEED – Gossip

1 Listen to three dialogues. In which dialogue do they gossip about the following?

1 a friend who's going to start work
2 two friends who have fallen out
3 two famous people who are going to get married

2 Match the parts of the sentences. Then listen again to check.

1 – d

1	Hey, you'll never guess	a	had a big argument.
2	I heard that	b	Kate and Darren?
3	You won't believe this,	c	told me.
4	A little bird	d	what I heard.
5	Have you heard about	e	but Marty's got a job.
6	Apparently, they	f	they've just got engaged.
7	Don't tell	g	say a word.
8	I won't	h	anyone, though!

3 Listen and repeat the sentences.

4 Complete the dialogue.

Chelsea (1) *Have you heard* about Maria Sparks and JJ West?
Ivan No.
Chelsea Well, I (2) … … they've just got engaged.
Ivan Really? That's interesting. You'll never guess (3) … … … .
Chelsea What?
Ivan (4) …, Marty's got a job. Don't (5) … … though.
Chelsea I won't (6) … … word.
Ivan And you (7) … … …, but Kate and Darren have broken up.
Chelsea How do you know?
Ivan (8) … … … told me.

5 Choose one of the following situations. Prepare and practise a dialogue.

1 Your school is organizing a surprise party.
2 Two famous people are going out together.
3 You saw a friend chatting up another friend.

WRITING – A news article

1 In pairs, answer the questions.

1 Does your school have a website? If so, what's on it?

A *Does our school have a website?*

B *Of course! Haven't you visited it?*

2 If not, do you think it would be a good idea? Why/Why not?

2 Read the article from a school newspaper on the Internet and answer the questions.

1 What did Jenny lose?
2 How did she lose it?
3 How did she get it back?

The Bridgetown School Times

All our news, written by us!

Jenny gets her violin back

Jenny Mills, from class 5B, was delighted to see her violin again last Friday. Jenny had lost her instrument two days earlier as she was travelling home from school.

The incident happened because Jenny fell asleep on the bus. When she woke up, the bus had gone past her stop, and she ran to get off – without her violin! By the time she noticed that it was missing, the bus had gone.

As soon as she got home, she rang the lost property office. Luckily, they phoned the next morning and told her that somebody had found it. Jenny admitted that she didn't think she would see it again.

Time connectors

*Jenny had lost her instrument **as** she was travelling home.*
***By the time** she noticed that her violin was missing, the bus had gone.*
***As soon as** she got home, she rang the lost property office.*

3 Complete the news stories with time connectors.

Cliff Chandler fell in the river (1) *as* he was cycling home from school. (2) … they saw the incident, some passers-by phoned the police. (3) … the police arrived, Cliff had swum to the side and was safe.

On Wednesday morning, Sarah Thomas received a letter. (4) … she saw it, she knew it was important. It said that she'd won first prize in an art competition. (5) … she was walking to school, she phoned her best friend to tell her about it. (6) … she got to school, everybody had heard the news.

Useful expressions

… was delighted to see …
… two days earlier …
The incident happened …
Luckily, …

4 Make notes. Then write an article for a school website.

Paragraph 1: A short summary of the news story.
Paragraph 2: More information about what happened.
Paragraph 3: What happened in the end.

5 Now read your work again. Can you find any errors?

My Portfolio Page 29

My Webpage

Review C

Units 7, 8, 9

1 Complete the sentences and match them with the pictures.

Mysteries wedding ~~newspaper~~ building

1. A *newspaper* awards ceremony. *3*
2. The opening of a … .
3. The '… of the World' conference.
4. A … reception.

2 Write the words in two minutes.

1. Eight types of building: *opera house, …*
2. Seven parts of a newspaper: *headline, …*
3. Six expressions that describe relationships: *go on a date, …*
4. Five words related to mysteries: *clues, …*

3 Use a word from each box to complete the sentences. Then listen and check.

do ~~get~~ have make

anything ~~married~~ a meal a speech

1. John's brother's *getting married* next month.
2. After the wedding, they're … … .
3. After the meal, John has to … … .
4. He doesn't want to … … wrong.

4 Look at his friend's advice. Write with *should* or *shouldn't*.

1. make notes first *You should make notes first.*
2. speak for too long
3. use a speech from the Internet
4. have a good time

SPEECH DAY

READING – Three speeches

①

②

③

1 **Read and listen. Match the speeches with the pictures.**

A I'd like to thank you all for coming to Paul and Eugenie's wedding. As you all know, they're moving to Canada next month. If I were Paul, I'd feel excited but also a little sad. All his friends and family are here and it's never easy to say goodbye. But you should both remember one thing: We'll always be here for you if you need us …

B When I was asked to come here today to officially open the new school library, I said it would be an honour. When the original building was destroyed by fire, the story made headlines in the local newspapers. In just a few hours our school was left without a very important collection of books. The new library is connected to other schools around the country …

C In a recent article, Doctor Jennifer Sanders said she had found evidence of the existence of extraterrestrials on our planet. She claimed that she had met three of these creatures and recorded an interview with them. In the interview, the visitors revealed that they had lived with us for the past 100 years. If the story is true, then Doctor Sanders will soon be the most famous scientist in the world …

2 **Find examples of the following in the texts.**

1. First conditional (two examples)
   If the story is true, then Doctor Sanders will soon be …
2. Second conditional (one example)
3. Reported speech (four examples)
4. Present passive (one example)
5. Past passive (three examples)

3 **Look at the speeches and write the questions. Then answer them.**

1. How / the speaker / feel / if he / be / Paul ?
   How would the speaker feel if he was Paul?
   He'd feel excited and sad.
2. What / Paul and Eugenie / remember ?
3. How / building / destroy ?
4. What / the school / leave / without ?
5. What / Doctor Sanders / find, according to a recent article ?
6. What / happen / if the story / true ?

4 **Write the verbs in the correct tense. Then match them with the speeches.**

admit meet make not work
sing make ~~die~~ know

1. 'The investigation revealed that no-one *had died* in the fire.' *B*
2. 'I knew Eugenie before she … Paul.'
3. 'The original structure … of wood.'
4. 'If I … any Canadian songs, I … one to you.'
5. 'However, if she … the story isn't true, she … again.'
6. 'Some newspapers are already … fun of her story.'

LISTENING – The interpreter

1 Listen and answer the questions.

1 Why did the aliens leave their planet?
There wasn't any water.
2 Did they travel for a long time?
3 Are the aliens dangerous?

2 Complete the sentences. Then listen and check.

a weather forecast ~~another planet~~
holiday trips hot dogs and tomato ketchup
TV or video games your beautiful planet

1 I'm from *another planet.*
2 I've fallen in love with …
3 We didn't have any …
4 We heard … on the ship's radio.
5 We don't want to destroy …
6 We'll organize …

3 Report the sentences in exercise 2.

1 – He said he was from another planet.

4 Choose the correct verb.

~~confirm~~ deny insist reveal

1 He *confirmed* that he was from another planet.
2 He … that he wanted to destroy our planet.
3 He … that he wanted to share their knowledge.
4 He … that they wouldn't hurt us.

SPEAKING – Be an interpreter

5 Talk to your partner for thirty seconds in your own language. Choose one of these topics.

a news story a TV show
a sports event last weekend

6 Your partner must try to translate what you say into English.

7 Your partner then writes a report of what you said.

PROJECT – Make a speech

1 Choose one of the situations.

you have won an award
a friend is moving to another country
you are speaking at the United Nations
you are opening a new sports centre

2 Make notes for the speech you're going to make. Include examples of reported speech, passives, *should/shouldn't* and first and second conditionals.

3 Practise your speech. When you are ready, make your speech to the class.

It's an honour to be here to…

SONG Rome wasn't built in a day

1 Use the words to complete the sentences. Then read and check.

Ambient British digital guest

1. Electronic musicians use … equipment.
2. … is a type of electronic music.
3. Morcheeba is a … band.
4. The band uses a … singer.

Electronic music

In the past, groups had to record albums in studios using real instruments. Now, they can make albums at home using digital equipment to reproduce instruments and create new sounds. Many music genres use this technology, especially chill-out, ambient and electronic dance music.
Morcheeba is a British band that plays chill-out electronic music. It was formed by brothers Paul and Ross Godfrey. They're joined by different female singers on their albums and on tour.

2 Read and listen to the song. What's its message?

a it takes a long time to build a city
b people should stop fighting
c it takes time to make a relationship work

3 Which phrases mean the same as …?

1. were made for each other *were meant to be*
2. you don't know how people will react
3. I'm in the middle of a fight/argument
4. we have to continue to work hard

Morcheeba

Chorus
You and me were meant to be
Walking free in harmony
One fine day we'll fly away
Don't you know that Rome wasn't built in a day

In this day and age it's so easy to stress
Cause people are strange and you can never second guess
In order to love child we got to be strong
I'm caught in the crossfire why can't we get along?

Chorus

I'm having a daydream, we're getting somewhere
I'm kissing your lips and running fingers through your hair
I'm as nervous as you 'bout making it right
Though we know we were wrong, we can't give up the fight
Oh no

Chorus

4 What do you think? True or false?

Electronic music isn't as good as music played on real instruments.
New technology's killing the music industry.
In the future, all music will be electronic.

You have to be a better musician to play …
The music industry's changing for the better/worse because …
In the future, people will probably continue to play …

GRAMMAR REFERENCE

WELCOME

Present simple: questions

- We form questions as follows:

  Verb *be*

  Are you Spanish?
  Is he new at this school?
  What's your name?

  Other verbs

  Do you **like** ice cream?
  Does she **live** near here?
  What school do you **go** to?

Adverbs of frequency

Adverbs of frequency

- We use the adverbs of frequency *always*, *usually*, *often*, *sometimes*, *occasionally*, *hardly ever* and *never* as follows:

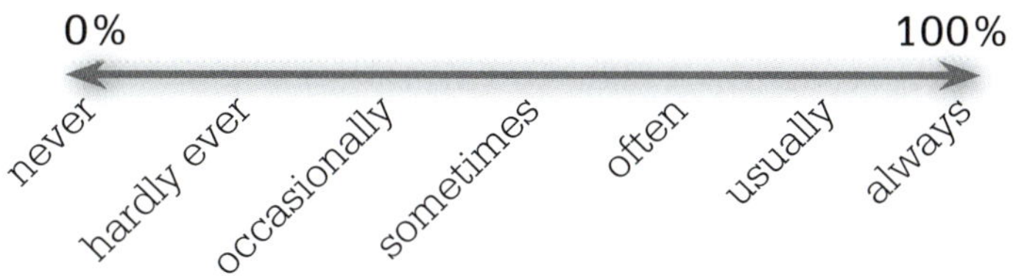

- We use adverbs of frequency with the present simple to say how regularly we do something. Adverbs of frequency go:

  – after the verb *be*.

  I'**m sometimes** lazy.

  – before other verbs.

  My friends **often come** round to my house at the weekend.

- We use *never* with an affirmative verb.

  We **never go** to the theatre.
  NOT We ~~don't~~ never go …

Frequency expressions

- We use longer expressions such as *once/ twice a week*, *three times a year* and *every weekend* at the end of the clause.

  Judith goes shopping **two or three times a month**.

how much/how many

- We use *how much* and *how many* to ask about quantity.

  How much money have you got?
  How many cars can you see?

Present simple v. present continuous

- We use the present continuous and present simple for different situations.

Present simple
For routines and habits. Samantha **washes** her hair daily.
For facts and things that are always true. December **isn't** a warm month in Europe.
With adverbs of frequency and other frequency expressions. I **go** to the park **every day**.
With state and sense verbs, e.g. *like*, *love*, *hate*, *want*, *know*, etc. We **like** tea. NOT We ~~are liking~~ tea.

Present continuous
For things that are happening now. **I'm talking** to John now.
With time expressions like *now*, *at the moment*. She**'s listening** to music **at the moment**.

Past simple: questions

- We form past simple questions of most verbs as follows:

  Where did they **go** on holiday?
  What sports **did** you **like** when you were young?

- We form short answers as follows:

  Did you **see** the match on Saturday?
  Yes, I **did**. / No, I **didn't**.

UNIT 1

like + *-ing* form

- We use the following verbs to talk about things we like and don't like doing:

love/like/enjoy don't mind prefer hate/can't stand	+ *-ing* form

I **can't stand watching** hockey.
Does Patricia **enjoy listening** to music?
What music **does** she **like listening** to?

- We use *doesn't mind* for the third person singular form of *don't mind*.
  Gary **doesn't mind picking** his brother up from school.
- We use *prefer* when we are talking about two options.
  Which **do** you **prefer doing**, **playing** computer games or **playing** football?

Spelling rules

Most verbs	talk try	+ *-ing*	talking trying
Verbs ending –e	use take	change *-e* to *-ing*	using taking
Verbs ending *–ie*	die tie	change *-ie* to *-y* + *-ing*	dying tying
Verbs ending consonant + vowel + consonant	forget swim	double consonant + *-ing*	forgetting swimming

Prepositions + *-ing* form

- After many prepositions, we use the *-ing* form.
  Tom bought the paper **before coming** home.
- These adjectives related to feelings are followed by different prepositions + *-ing* form.

Adjective	Preposition
good, hopeless	at
afraid	of
keen	on
interested	in
serious	about

I'm **hopeless at learning** languages.
Ian is **interested in studying** Law.

Verbs of ambition + infinitive

- We use the following verbs to talk about our hopes and plans for the future.

want hope plan 'd like wouldn't like	+ infinitive with *to*

I **want to travel** to Asia one day.
Phil **hopes to work** in the theatre.
What **do** you **plan to do**?
They**'d like to take** a year off before they start their course.
We **wouldn't like to fail** the exam.

have to: present

Affirmative	Negative
I have to go. You have to go. He has to go. She has to go. It has to go.	I don't have to go. You don't have to go. He doesn't have to go. She doesn't have to go. It doesn't have to go.
We have to go. You have to go. They have to go.	We don't have to go. You don't have to go. They don't have to go.

Questions
Do I have to go? Do you have to go? Does he have to go? Does she have to go? Does it have to go?
Do we have to go? Do you have to go? Do they have to go?

Short answers	
Affirmative	Negative
Yes, I do. Yes, you do. Yes, he does. Yes, she does. Yes, it does.	No, I don't. No, you don't. No, he doesn't. No, she doesn't. No, it doesn't.
Yes, we do. Yes, you do. Yes, they do.	No, we don't. No, you don't. No, they don't.

- We use *have to* to express an obligation or necessity.
- We use *have to* for actions that are necessary because of a rule or an order or because the situation requires them.
  You **have to do** your homework.
  You **have to start** playing very young if you want to be the best.
- We use *don't have to* for an absence of obligation rather than prohibition.
  You **don't have to be** very strong to play this sport. (= it isn't necessary)
- We use question words to make *wh-* questions.
  Why do we **have to hold** it like that?
- In short answers, we repeat the auxiliary *do/does*.
  Do you **have to go** to choir practice?
  Yes, I **do**. NOT Yes, ~~I have (to)~~.

have to: past

- The past simple form of *have to* is *had to*.

Affirmative	Negative
I had to go. You had to go. He had to go. She had to go. It had to go.	I didn't have to go. You didn't have to go. He didn't have to go. She didn't have to go. It didn't have to go.
We had to go. You had to go. They had to go.	We didn't have to go. You didn't have to go. They didn't have to go.

Questions
Did I have to go? Did you have to go? Did he have to go? Did she have to go? Did it have to go?
Did we have to go? Did you have to go? Did they have to go?

Short answers	
Affirmative	Negative
Yes, I did. Yes, you did. Yes, he did. Yes, she did. Yes, it did.	No, I didn't. No, you didn't. No, he didn't. No, she didn't. No, it didn't.
Yes, we did. Yes, you did. Yes, they did.	No, we didn't. No, you didn't. No, they didn't.

- We use question words to make *wh-* questions.
  Why did we **have to practise** so much?

UNIT 2

Past simple v. past continuous

Past simple

- For a list of irregular verbs, see p. 120 in the Workbook.

Affirmative	Negative
I talked. You talked. He talked. She talked. It talked.	I didn't talk. You didn't talk. He didn't talk. She didn't talk. It didn't talk.
We talked. You talked. They talked.	We didn't talk. You didn't talk. They didn't talk.

Questions
Did I talk? Did you talk? Did he talk? Did she talk? Did it talk?
Did we talk? Did you talk? Did they talk?

Short answers	
Affirmative	Negative
Yes, I did. Yes, you did. Yes, he did. Yes, she did. Yes, it did.	No, I didn't. No, you didn't. No, he didn't. No, she didn't. No, it didn't.
Yes, we did. Yes, you did. Yes, they did.	No, we didn't. No, you didn't. No, they didn't.

Past continuous

Affirmative
I was eating. You were eating. He was eating. She was eating. It was eating.
We were eating. You were eating. They were eating.

Negative	
Full form	Contracted form
I was not eating. You were not eating. He was not eating. She was not eating. It was not eating.	I wasn't eating. You weren't eating. He wasn't eating. She wasn't eating. It wasn't eating.
We were not eating. You were not eating. They were not eating.	We weren't eating. You weren't eating. They weren't eating.

Questions
Was I eating? Were you eating? Was he eating? Was she eating? Was it eating?
Were we eating? Were you eating? Were they eating?

Short answers	
Affirmative	Negative
Yes, I was. Yes, you were. Yes, he was. Yes, she was. Yes, it was.	No, I wasn't. No, you weren't. No, he wasn't. No, she wasn't. No, it wasn't.
Yes, we were. Yes, you were. Yes, they were.	No, we weren't. No, you weren't. No, they weren't.

- Here is a summary of past simple and past continuous uses:

Past simple	Past continuous
For complete actions in the past. Diana **stayed** with Karen for several weeks.	For actions that were in progress at a specific time in the past. Diana **was staying** with Karen last week.
After *when* in a past continuous sentence to introduce a second action. I was talking on the phone **when** you **arrived** home.	After *when* or *while* to describe two actions that were happening at the same time. I was talking on the phone **when/while** you **were cooking** dinner.

- We can reverse the order of clauses beginning with *when* or *while*.
  When I turned round, he was looking the other way.
  While I was trying to study, you were playing loud music.

used to

Affirmative	Negative
I used to swim. You used to swim. He used to swim. She used to swim. It used to swim.	I didn't use to swim. You didn't use to swim. He didn't use to swim. She didn't use to swim. It didn't use to swim.
We used to swim. You used to swim. They used to swim.	We didn't use to swim. You didn't use to swim. They didn't use to swim.

- We use *used to* + infinitive to talk about habits and routines in the past.
  Peter **used to play** football when he was seven.
- We can use this expression with frequency expressions, such as *once a week*, *every Friday*, etc.
  I **used to walk** my dog twice a day.

used to: questions

- *Used to* can also appear in questions.
  Did you **use to collect** stamps?

Short answers	
Affirmative	Negative
Yes, I did. Yes, you did. Yes, he did. Yes, she did. Yes, it did.	No, I didn't. No, you didn't. No, he didn't. No, she didn't. No, it didn't.
Yes, we did. Yes, you did. Yes, they did.	No, we didn't. No, you didn't. No, they didn't.

Did you and Jean **use to live** in London?
Yes, **we did**.

- We use question words to make *wh-* questions.
  Where did you **use to go** on holiday?

UNIT 3

Present perfect with *just*

- We use *just* with affirmative sentences and questions in the present perfect to emphasize that something happened immediately before the moment of speaking.
- The position of *just* is before the past participle.
  I've just finished making the dinner.
  Have you **just realized** what time it is?

already and *yet*

- We use *already* in affirmative sentences and questions to talk about something that has happened before it was expected to.
- The position of *already* is before the past participle.
  Mr Smith **has already arrived**. He's twenty minutes early.
- We use *yet* in negative sentences and questions to talk about something that was expected to happen but which hasn't happened at the time of speaking.
- The position of *yet* is at the end of the clause.
  Robert Gable **hasn't called yet**. We're still waiting.
  Have you **met** Billie **yet**?

Present perfect with *for/since*

- We often use the question *How long?* with the present perfect to find out how much time has passed between the beginning of an action and now.
  How long has Gina **worked** at this company? (= Gina is still working there.)
- If we ask the question in the past simple (How long did Gina work at this company?) it suggests that Gina is not working there now.

- We often reply to present perfect, questions beginning *How long?* with the present perfect + *for/since*.
  - **for** + period of time, e.g. a day, a week, a month, a year, several weeks/months/ years
  - **since** + specific time, day, date, year or clause
    She's worked here **for a few months**.
    She's worked here **since July**.
    She's worked here **since Harry left**.
- We can answer *How long?* questions with full sentences or just the *for/since* expression itself.
  How long have you **had** that coat?
  For a couple of months.
  Since my birthday.
  Since Jamie gave it to me.

UNIT 4

Comparatives and superlatives

Spelling rules

		Comparative	Superlative
Short adjective small	+ *-er/-est*	smaller	the smallest
Adjective ending in *-e* large	+ *-r/-st*	larger	the largest
Short adjective ending in vowel + consonant, except *-w* big	double the consonant + *-er/-est*	bigger	the biggest
Adjective of two or more syllables modern expensive	*more/most* + adjective	more modern more expensive	the most modern the most expensive
Adjective ending in consonant + *-y* early	change *-y* to *-i* + *-er/-est*	earlier	the earliest
Irregular adjective good bad far	Irregular	better worse farther/ further	the best the worst the farthest/ furthest

- We use comparative adjectives to compare two people, animals or things.
  These flowers are **nicer** than those.
- We always follow the comparative adjective with *than*, not *that*.
  NOT These flowers are nicer ~~that~~ those.
- We use superlative adjectives to compare three or more people, animals or things.
  The flowers over there are **the nicest ones** in the shop.
- We use the preposition *in*, not *of*, for the place where the compared things are.
  NOT The flowers over there are the nicest ones ~~of~~ the shop.

(not) as ... as ...

- We use *(not) as* + adjective + *as* to compare two people, things or places that have the same qualities.
- We can use this expression in affirmative and negative sentences and in questions.
  My house **is** nearly **as old as** yours.
  Hilary **isn't as tall as** me.
  Is the Thames **as wide as** the Seine?

too and *not enough* with adjectives

***too* + adjective**

- The expression *too* + adjective has a similar meaning to *too much* or *too many*.
  I don't want to buy that one. It's **too expensive**. (= it costs more money than I wanted to pay.)

- While *too much* and *too many* are followed by a noun, *too* on its own is followed by an adjective.
Let's go home. It's **too crowded** here.
(= There are too many people.)

(not) enough + adjective

- The expression adjective + *(not) enough* means 'less than we need'.
Is your room **warm enough**? (= Do you need more heating?)
- Be careful with the position of *enough*. It goes after the adjective, not before.
NOT ~~enough warm~~
- We can also use this expression in the negative.
I can't get to sleep. I'm **not tired enough**.

Sense verbs

- We use the following sense verbs to describe what we can see, hear, feel, taste and smell:

look sound feel taste smell	+ adjective

This cheese **tastes wonderful**.
What's this music? It **sounds great**.

- We can use the same verbs + *like* + noun to make a direct comparison with another thing.
This material **feels like** cotton.
- Don't forget that we don't use *a* or *an* before an uncountable noun.
This cheese **tastes like cream**.
She's beautiful. She **looks like a model**.

Verbs of probability

- We use the verbs *must, could, might, may* and *can't* to talk about different degrees of probability.

0%		100%
can't	could/may/might	must

That man **can't be** Juan. He doesn't look like him.
That's a strange animal. It **could/may/might be** a cat, but it looks too big.
What language are they speaking? We're in Brazil, so it **must be** Portuguese.

UNIT 5

Relative pronouns

- Relative clauses define the place, person or object that the speaker is talking about. They are introduced by the relative pronouns *who*, *which*, *that*, *whose* and *where*.
The man **who** I was talking to.
The dog **which** we adopted.
The house **that** we lived in.
The woman **whose** jacket I borrowed.
The place **where** I got married.
- We can use *that* instead of *who*, *which* and *where*, but not *whose*.
The man **that** I was talking to.
The dog **that** we adopted.
The place **that** I got married.
- We do not use commas to separate the relative clause from the rest of the sentence.
The man **who/that** works in the newsagent's is Austrian.
- In the sentence above, the relative pronoun *who/that* refers to the subject of the sentence ('the man').
- We do not use a pronoun (e.g. *him*, *them*) in addition to *who*, *which* or *that*.
She is the woman who you met at the party.
NOT She is the woman who you met ~~her~~ at the party.

Omitting *who*, *which* and *that*

- When the relative pronouns *who/which/that/where* refer to the object of the relative clause, we can omit them.

The woman **who** we spoke to was Joe's mother.
OR
The woman we spoke to was Joe's mother.

- We never use *which* to refer to a person.
  The girl **who/that** is reading the newspaper is in my class.
  NOT The girl ~~which~~ …

Subject and object questions

- Subject questions do not need an auxiliary verb.

Subject question	Object question
Who helped you?	Who did you help?
What gave you the idea?	What did you give to Monica?

- In the questions above, we change the order of the sentence depending on whether *who* or *what* is the subject or object of the sentence.
- When *who* or *what* is the subject, they do not have an auxiliary but are immediately followed by the main verb.
  Who did you meet yesterday?
  What did she have for lunch?
- When *who* or *what* is the object of the sentence, they are followed by the normal word order for a question: auxiliary and the subject + infinitive.
  Who have **you** told?
  What does **she** look like?
- If the main verb has a preposition, this usually goes at the end.
  Who are you waiting **for**?
  NOT ~~For~~ who are you waiting?

UNIT 6

Future forms

will

- We use *will/won't* to talk about:
  - future facts in general
    I'**ll ask** about Joanne when I see her mother.
  - predictions
    There **will be** world famine by 2050.
    We **won't have** enough to eat.
    Petrol **will probably become** more expensive this year.
    There **probably won't be** a financial crisis. Things are getting better.

going to

- We use *be + going to*:
  - To describe an intention.
    I'm going to start keeping a diary.
  - To talk about a future plan.
    Mark and James **are** both **going to study** in America next summer.
  - To make a prediction about the future based on evidence in the present.
    I feel really strange. I think **I'm going to faint**.
  - We do not use the present simple to describe an intention or a decision to do something.
    I'm hungry. **I'm going** to eat something.
    NOT ~~I go~~ to eat something.

Present Continuous

- We can use this tense to talk about future plans that have already been confirmed, such as dates, timetables, planned events, etc.
- We often use a future time expression, in order to make it clear that the action is not happening now.
  Our aunt and uncle **are visiting** us **next week**.
  The bus timetable **is changing soon**.

- If we use a verb expressing opinion, such as *think*, before a verb in the future simple, *going to*, or present continuous, we form the negative with the first verb.
  I don't think he's coming to the party.
  NOT ~~I think he isn't~~ coming to the party.
  I don't think it's going to rain.
  NOT ~~I think it's not~~ going to rain.

will and *might*

- We use *will*, *will probably*, *probably won't* and *might* + infinitive to make our opinions and predictions more certain or less certain.
  There **might be** a problem with food resources in twenty years.
  (= but I'm not sure)
  Those countries are very unstable.
  The violence **will probably get** worse.
  (= it looks very likely)
  Shops **probably won't sell** video cassettes in five years' time.
  (= it looks very likely)
  More and more people **will work** from home. (= I'm certain of this)

First conditional

- We use conditional clauses to describe situations that we think are possible in both the present and the future.

Conditional clause	Main clause
If you do more exercise,	you'll lose weight.

- The meaning does not change if we reverse the order of the clauses. We do not use a comma to separate the clauses when the main clause comes first.

Main clause	Conditional clause
You'll lose weight	if you do more exercise.

- Instead of using *will* in the main clause, we can use other modal verbs such as *might* and *will be able to*.
  If we don't do something soon, we **might end up** destroying our planet.
  We **won't be able to swim** in the sea if it becomes too polluted.
  People **will probably live** a lot longer if our scientific knowledge improves.

- In a conditional clause, *if* is followed by the present simple, even though the verb refers to the future.
  If you **want** to come, you**'ll have** to be there by 7.30.
  NOT If you ~~will~~ want to come ...

UNIT 7

Second conditional

- We use second conditional clauses to describe situations that are imaginary or unreal.

Conditional clause	Main clause
If you came with us,	you'd have a fantastic time.

If you **lived** in California, how **would** you **spend** your days? (= imaginary situation)

- As with first conditional sentences, we can reverse the order of the clauses.

Main clause	Conditional clause
What would you do	if you won the lottery?

- When using the verb *be* in the *if* clause, we can use *were* for all persons, including the first and third persons singular. However, *was* is more frequent nowadays.
  If I **was/were** a good swimmer, I'd try to swim the English Channel.

should/shouldn't

- We use *should* and *shouldn't* + infinitive to give advice.
  You **should ask** the doctor about this.
  She **shouldn't eat** so much chocolate.

- We can say *I think* before we give advice with *should*.
  I think you should find somewhere else to live.

Second conditional for advice

- We can use the second conditional form *If I were you, I'd* + infinitive as a way of giving advice.
My flatmate is a very difficult person and keeps starting arguments.
If I were you, I'd find a new flat.

First v. second conditional

- Here's a summary of the first and second conditional forms:

First conditional (= possible situation)	**If** you **take** these tablets, you**'ll feel** much better.
Second conditional (= imaginary situation)	**If** you **had** more money, you**'d be able to** go on holiday.

UNIT 8

Passive: present and past

	Affirmative	Negative
Present passive	This bag is made of real leather.	Rolls Royce cars aren't made in the UK.

Lemons **are grown** in Greece.
The two parts of the machine **aren't connected**.

	Affirmative	Negative
Past passive	People were advised to stay in.	The shoes weren't repaired on time.

Everyone **was given** a present.
Richard and Ken **weren't interviewed** for the job.

- We use the passive voice when we want to give greater importance to the action and its object than to the agent who performs the action.
My bag **was stolen** last week.

Present simple active → passive

Active: They **produce** wine and olive oil in Spain.
Passive: Wine and olive oil **are produced** in Spain.

Past simple active → passive

Active: They **didn't finish** the work on time.
Passive: The work **wasn't finished** on time.

- We can use the preposition *by* to introduce the subject of the active verb, the agent, in the passive voice.

Active: John Logie Baird **invented** the television.
Passive: The television **was invented by** John Logie Baird.

- We omit *by* + the agent when it is not important to know who did the action.
Cycling on the pavement is prohibited.

Passive: questions

	Questions	Short answers
Present passive	Is this bag made of real leather?	Yes, it is. / No, it isn't.

Are lemons **grown** in Greece?
Yes, they **are**.
Are the two parts of the machine **connected**?
No, they **aren't**.

	Questions	Short answers
Past passive	Were people advised to stay in?	Yes, they were. / No, they weren't.

Was John **given** a present?
Yes, he **was**.
Were Richard and Ken **interviewed** for the job?
No, they **weren't**.

- We can also use question words to make *wh-* questions.
Where are lemons **grown**?
Why weren't Richard and Ken **interviewed** for the job?

UNIT 9

Past perfect

Affirmative	
Full form	**Contracted form**
I had passed. You had passed. He had passed. She had passed. It had passed.	I'd passed. You'd passed. He'd passed. She'd passed. It'd passed.
We had passed. You had passed. They had passed.	We'd passed. You'd passed. They'd passed.

Negative	
Full form	**Contracted form**
I had not passed. You had not passed. He had not passed. She had not passed. It had not passed.	I hadn't passed. You hadn't passed. He hadn't passed. She hadn't passed. It hadn't passed.
We had not passed. You had not passed. They had not passed.	We hadn't passed. You hadn't passed. They hadn't passed.

- We use the past perfect to talk about something that happened before something else in the past.
  Marie **had left** the office when I called her.
  (= Marie left the office, then I called her)
  When Colin **had finished** his dinner, he went to watch TV. (= Colin finished his dinner, then he went to watch TV)
- We can also use the past perfect to explain a situation or give a reason.
  I was nervous because I **hadn't driven** on the motorway before.

Past perfect: questions

Questions
Had I passed? Had you passed? Had he passed? Had she passed? Had it passed?
Had we passed? Had you passed? Had they passed?

Short answers	
Affirmative	**Negative**
Yes, I had. Yes, you had. Yes, he had. Yes, she had. Yes, it had.	No, I hadn't. No, you hadn't. No, he hadn't. No, she hadn't. No, it hadn't.
Yes, we had. Yes, you had. Yes, they had.	No, we hadn't. No, you hadn't. No, they hadn't.

Had you ever **been** to Benidorm before this summer?
No, I **hadn't**.

- Past perfect questions are used in the same situations as the affirmative and negative forms.

Reported speech

- Reported speech is used to repeat what another person said without using their exact words.

Direct speech	Reported speech
He told me: 'I'm worried.'	He told me (that) he was worried.
He said: 'I'm worried.'	He said (that) he was worried.

- When the verb introducing the reported speech ('reporting verb') is in the past, the following changes occur:

Direct speech	Reported speech
Present simple She said: 'I **work** in London.'	Past simple She said (that) she **worked** in London.
Present continuous He said: '**I'm completing** a project.'	Past continuous He said (that) he **was completing** a project.
Present perfect She said: '**I've broken** my arm.'	Past perfect She said (that) she **had broken** her arm.
Past simple He said: 'I **talked** to them.'	Past perfect He said (that) he **had talked** to them.
will + infinitive He said: 'I **will arrive** home early.'	would + infinitive He said (that) he **would arrive** home early.

- We also change modal verbs:

Direct speech	Reported speech
can She said: 'I **can speak** German.'	*could* She said (that) she **could speak** German.
will He said: '**I'll be** home soon.'	*would* He said (that) he **would be** home soon.
must/have (got) to She said: 'You **must leave**.'	*had to* She said (that) I **had to leave**.
may He said: 'It **may snow** later.'	*might* He said (that) it **might snow** later.

say and *tell*

- *Say* and *tell* are the most common reporting verbs.
- If we use *told*, we must follow it with an object pronoun.
  She **told me** (that) she was going away.
  NOT She ~~told (that)~~ she was going away.
- However, this is not the case with *said*.
  NOT She said ~~me~~ that …
- There are other reporting verbs that we can use apart from *say* and *tell*. These include: *admit*, *claim*, *confirm*, *deny*, *insist*, *reveal*. These verbs are like *say*: they can't be followed by an object pronoun.
  They **admitted (that)** they'd committed the crime.
  NOT They admitted ~~me~~ (that) …

WORD LIST

WELCOME

- Expressions

these days	/ðiːz deɪz/
in common	/ɪn 'kɒmən/

UNIT 1

Performing arts

audience	/'ɔːdiəns/
audition	/ɔː'dɪʃn/
ballet	/'bæleɪ/
choreographer	/kɒri'ɒgrəfə/
conductor	/kən'dʌktə/
live music	/laɪv 'mjuːzɪk/
orchestra	/'ɔːkɪstrə/
performance	/pə'fɔːməns/
play	/pleɪ/
playwright	/'pleɪraɪt/
rehearsal	/rɪ'hɜːsl/
stage	/steɪdʒ/

Musical instruments

accordion	/ə'kɔːdiən/
cello	/'tʃeləʊ/
clarinet	/klærɪ'net/
double bass	/'dʌbl beɪs/
flute	/fluːt/
recorder	/rɪ'kɔːdə/
saxophone	/'sæksəfəʊn/
steel drums	/stiːl drʌmz/
tambourine	/tæmbə'riːn/
trombone	/trɒm'bəʊn/
trumpet	/'trʌmpɪt/
violin	/vaɪə'lɪn/

English you need

- Be a critic

I was expecting it to be really boring.

It was absolutely amazing.

I really enjoyed the music.

The best thing about it was the choreography.

Everyone says it's great.

I thought the *Harry Potter* books were better.

I found this book a little slow.

I was disappointed by the ending.

Other words

- Nouns

acting	/'æktɪŋ/
media	/'miːdiə/
part (in a play)	/pɑːt/
performing arts	/pə'fɔːmɪŋ ɑːts/
publisher	/'pʌblɪʃə/
spare time	/speə taɪm/

- Verbs

publish	/'pʌblɪʃ/
rehearse	/rɪ'hɜːs/

- Adjectives

fictional	/'fɪkʃənl/
former	/'fɔːmə/
talented	/'tæləntɪd/

- Expressions

behind the scenes	/bɪ'haɪnd ðə siːnz/
be keen on something	/biː kiːn ɒn sʌmθɪŋ/

UNIT 2

Places in a village

bridge	/brɪdʒ/
church	/tʃɜːtʃ/
crossroads	/'krɒsrəʊdz/

farmhouse	/'fɑːmhaʊs/
fence	/fens/
field	/fiːld/
gate	/geɪt/
hill	/hɪl/
path	/pɑːθ/
signpost	/'saɪnpəʊst/
stream	/striːm/
wood	/wʊd/

Materials

glass	/glɑːs/
leather	/'leðə/
metal	/'metl/
plastic	/'plæstɪk/
silk	/sɪlk/
silver	/'sɪlvə/
wooden	/'wʊdn/
woollen	/'wʊlən/

English you need

- Ask permission

Can I go?

No, you can't.

I'm sorry, but no.

Is it all right if I give it to you on Monday?

I suppose so.

Yes, OK.

Do you mind if I paint it black?

All right, you can if you like.

Other words

- Nouns

ghost	/gəʊst/
glass	/glɑːs/
landlady	/'lændleɪdi/
local	/'ləʊkl/
possessions	/pə'zeʃənz/
stranger	/'streɪndʒə/

- Verbs

approach	/ə'prəʊtʃ/
extend	/ɪk'stend/
hide	/haɪd/
scream	/skriːm/

- Adjectives

atmospheric	/ætməs'ferɪk/
cheeky	/'tʃiːki/
eerie	/'ɪəri/
haunted	/'hɔːntɪd/
picturesque	/pɪktʃə'resk/

- Adverbs

nowadays	/'naʊədeɪz/

UNIT 3

Travel

book a ticket	/buːk ə 'tɪkɪt/
go hiking	/gəʊ 'haɪkɪŋ/
go sightseeing	/gəʊ 'saɪtsiːɪŋ/
hire a bike	/haɪə ə baɪk/
pack a rucksack (UK) backpack (US)	/pæk ə 'rʌksæk 'bækpæk/
plan a route	/plæn ə ruːt/
set off on a journey	/set ɒf ɒn ə 'dʒɜːni/
stay at a youth hostel	/steɪ ət ə juːθ 'hɒstəl/

British v. American English

British

film	/fɪlm/
football	/'fʊtbɔːl/
ground floor	/graʊnd flɔː/
holiday	/'hɒlədeɪ/
lift	/lɪft/
mobile	/'məʊbaɪl/
pavement	/'peɪvmənt/

petrol	/'petrəl/
rubbish	/'rʌbɪʃ/
trousers	/'traʊzəz/
underground	/'ʌndəgraʊnd/
trainers	/'treɪnəz/

American

movie	/'mu:vi/
soccer	/'sɒkə/
first floor	/fɜ:st flɔ:/
vacation	/veɪ'keɪʃn/
elevator	/'elɪveɪtə/
cell phone	/sel fəʊn/
sidewalk	/'saɪdwɔ:k/
gas	/gæs/
garbage	/'gɑ:bɪdʒ/
pants	/pænts/
subway	/'sʌbweɪ/
sneakers	/'sni:kəz/

English you need

• Apologize

I'm sorry.
I said I'm sorry.
I'm sorry I'm late.
It wasn't my fault.
It was an accident.
That's all right.
Don't worry about it.
I'm really sorry about your T-shirt.

Other words

• Nouns

camp	/kæmp/
custom	/'kʌstəm/
greetings	/'gri:tɪŋz/
harbour	/'hɑ:bə/
journey	/'dʒɜ:ni/
rollerblading	/'rəʊləbleɪdɪŋ/
trip	/trɪp/

• Verbs

eat out	/i:t aʊt/
pause	/pɔ:z/
suit	/su:t/
travel	/'trævəl/

• Adjectives

amazing	/ə'meɪzɪŋ/
part-time	/pɑ:t'taɪm/

• Expressions

by the way	/baɪ ɵə weɪ/
Greetings from ...!	/'gri:tɪŋz frəm/
get a view of	/get ə vju: əv/
make friends with	/meɪk frendz wɪð/
plenty of	/'plenti əv/

UNIT 4

Shopping

bargain	/'bɑ:gɪn/
basket	/bɑ:skɪt/
changing rooms	/'tʃeɪndʒɪŋ ru:mz/
checkout	/'tʃekaʊt/
counter	/'kaʊntə/
receipt	/rɪ'si:t/
shopper	/'ʃɒpə/
the sales	/ðə seɪlz/
till	/tɪl/
trolley	/'trɒli/

Advertising

advertising campaign	/'ædvətaɪzɪŋ kæm'peɪn/
launch	/lɔ:ntʃ/
logo	/'ləʊgəʊ/
market research	/'mɑ:kət ri'sɜ:tʃ/
product	/'prɑdʌkt/
promote	/prə'məʊt/
slogan	/'sləʊgən/

TV commercial	/tiː'viː kə'mɜːʃl/

English you need

• Persuade somebody

No way!

Please, go on!

I'd prefer to stay at home.

Oh, come on.

Don't be boring!

Oh, all right then. I give in.

Other words

• Nouns

colour scheme	/'kʌlə skiːm/
discovery	/dɪs'kʌvəri/
survey	/'sɜːveɪ/
trap	/træp/
trick	/trɪk/

• Verbs

browse	/braʊz/
go on	/gəʊ ɒn/
look like	/lʊk laɪk/
persuade	/pə'sweɪd/
reveal	/rɪ'viːl/

• Adjectives

entitled	/ən'taɪtld/
everyday	/'evrideɪ/
on offer	/ɒn 'ɒfə/
predictable	/prɪ'dɪktəbl/
uncomfortable	/ʌn'kʌmftəbl/

UNIT 5

Identity

bank account number	/bæŋk ə'kaʊnt 'nʌmbə/
debit card	/'debɪt kɑːd/
driving licence	/'draɪvɪŋ 'laɪsəns/
fingerprint	/'fɪŋgəprɪnt/
identity card	/aɪ'dentəti kɑːd/
laptop	/'læptɒp/
password	/'pɑːswɜːd/
personal identification number (PIN)	/'pɜːsənəl aɪdentɪfɪ'keɪʃn 'nʌmbə/
signature	/'sɪgnətʃə/
user name	/'juːzə neɪm/

Verbs for historical events

attempt	/ə'tempt/
beat	/biːt/
become	/bɪ'kʌm/
break out	/breɪk aʊt/
fight for	/faɪt fɔː/
found	/faʊnd/
shoot	/ʃuːt/
sink	/sɪŋk/

English you need

• Express your view

I think it's good because you can meet people.

I don't agree.

In my opinion it's important to meet people.

Do you really think so?

What do you think?

I'm not sure.

I agree.

I suppose so.

Other words

• Nouns

CCTV (closed-circuit television)	/siːsiːtiː'viː/
profile	/'prəʊfaɪl/
social networking site	/'səʊʃl 'netwɜːkɪŋ saɪt/
twin	/twɪn/

• Verbs

inherit	/ɪn'herɪt/

- Verbs

inherit	/ɪn'herɪt/
post (on a website)	/pəʊst/
reckon	/'rekn/
remove	/rɪ'muːv/

- Adjectives

reliable	/rɪ'laɪəbl/

- Expressions

treat somebody like a	/triːt 'sʌmbədi laɪk ə/

UNIT 6

Natural disasters

desertification	/dɪ'zɜːtɪfɪkeɪʃən/
drought	/draʊt/
earthquake	/'ɜːθkweɪk/
flood	/flʌd/
forest fire	/'fɔːrɪst faɪə/
glacier	/'glæsiə/
hurricane	/'hʌrɪkən/
iceberg	/'aɪsbɜːg/
tornado	/tɔː'neɪdəʊ/
volcanic eruption	/vɒl'kænɪk ɪ'rʌpʃn/

Crime

burglar	/'bɜːglə/
burglary	/'bɜːgləri/
burgle	/'bɜːgl/
crime	/kraɪm/
criminal	/'krɪmɪnl/
illegal	/ɪ'liːgl/
legal	/'liːgl/
legalize	/'liːgəlaɪz/
piracy	/'paɪrəsi/
rob	/rɒb/
robber	/'rɒbə/
robbery	/'rɒbəri/
shoplifter	/'ʃɒplɪftə/
shoplifting	/'ʃɒplɪftɪŋ/
steal	/stiːl/
theft	/θeft/
thief	/θiːf/

English you need

- Make a presentation

Today I'd like to talk to you about a person I admire.

I'm going to start by telling you about her character.

So, I've told you about why I became interested.

Now let's look at how I found information.

What does this mean? Well, to give you an example …

To conclude, I'd like to summarize the key points.

Firstly, scientists still don't know the risks.

Secondly, phone companies want us to spend money.

Have you got any questions?

Other words

- Nouns

degree	/dɪ'griː/
global warming	/'gləʊbl 'wɔːmɪŋ/
leaflet	/'liːflət/
rainforest	/'reɪnfɒrɪst/
thickness	/'θɪknəs/

- Verbs

cycle	/'saɪkl/
melt	/melt/
petition	/pə'tɪʃn/
link	/lɪŋk/
promote	/prə'məʊt/

- Adjectives

charitable	/'tʃærɪtəbl/
thrilled	/θrɪld/

- Expressions

be related to	/biː rɪ'leɪtɪd tə/
take action	/teɪk 'ækʃn/

UNIT 7

Relationships

break up	/breɪk ʌp/
chat up	/tʃæt ʌp/
fall in love	/fɔːl ɪn lʌv/
fall out	/fɔːl aʊt/
get back together	/get bæk tə'geðə/
get engaged	/get ɪn'geɪdʒd/
get married	/get 'mærid/
get on	/get ɒn/
get over	/get 'əʊvə/
go on a date	/gəʊ ɒn ə deɪt/
go out	/gəʊ aʊt/
make up	/meɪk ʌp/

Collocations with *have*, *do* and *make*

do nothing	/duː 'nʌθɪŋ/
do something wrong	/duː 'sʌmθɪŋ rɒŋ/
have a conversation	/hæv ə kɒnvə'seɪʃn/
have a good time	/hæv ə guːd taɪm/
have a party	/hæv ə 'paːti/
have an argument	/hæv ən 'aːgjʊmənt/
make a mistake	/meɪk ə mɪs'teɪk/
make an effort	/meɪk ən 'efət/
make an excuse	/meɪk ən ɪk'skjuːs/
make fun of somebody	/meɪk fʌn əv 'svmbədi/

English you need

- Be a mediator

Hey! What's going on?

Emma, what happened exactly?

Is that right, John?

Emma, let him finish.

That isn't fair.

Why don't you record the music programme?

That way, you can both see what you want.

Does that seem fair, Emma?

Other words

- Nouns

blind date	/blaɪnd deɪt/
dispute	/dɪ'spjuːt/
score	/skɔː/
training	/'treɪnɪŋ/
volunteer	/vɒlən'tɪə/

- Verbs

joke	/dʒəʊk/
vandalize	/'vændəlaɪz/

- Expressions

both sides	/bəʊθ saɪdz/
If I were you,...	/ɪf aɪ wə juː/
make a mess	/meɪk ə mes/
tell lies	/tel laɪz/
You must be joking!	/juː mʌst bi 'dʒəʊkɪŋ/

UNIT 8

Monuments

church	/tʃɜːtʃ/
lighthouse	/'laɪthaʊs/
monastery	/'mɒnəstri/
mosque	/mɒsk/
opera house	/'ɒprə haʊs/
palace	/'pælɪs/
pyramid	/'pɪrəmɪd/
skyscraper	/'skaɪskreɪpə/
temple	/'templ/
wall	/wɔːl/

Mysteries

case	/keɪs/
clue	/kluː/
evidence	/ˈevɪdəns/
fact	/fækt/
mystery	/ˈmɪstəri/
theory	/ˈθɪəri/

English you need

- Express doubt

I don't know.

I'm not sure if that's true.

I doubt if they knew about mercury.

I doubt it.

Do you really think so?

I'm not convinced that they'll play them.

I'm not sure.

I don't know if I want to go alone.

Other words

- Nouns

capsule	/ˈkæpsjuːl/
dome	/dəʊm/
location	/ləʊˈkeɪʃən/
mayor	/meə/
site	/saɪt/
steel	/stiːl/
tomb	/tuːm/

- Verbs

go round	/gəʊ raʊnd/
surround	/səˈraʊnd/

- Adjectives

life-sized	/ˈlaɪfsaɪzd/

- Expressions

Typical!	/ˈtɪpɪkl/

UNIT 9

Newspapers

caption	/ˈkæpʃn/
cartoon	/kɑːˈtuːn/
front page	/frʌnt peɪdʒ/
headline	/ˈhedlaɪn/
horoscope	/ˈhɒrəskəʊp/
local news	/ˈləʊkl njuːz/
sports section	/spɔːts ˈsekʃn/
weather forecast	/ˈweðə ˈfɔːkɑːst/
world news	/wɜːld njuːz/

Reporting verbs

admit	/ədˈmɪt/
claim	/kleɪm/
confirm	/kənˈfɜːm/
deny	/dɪˈnaɪ/
insist	/ɪnˈsɪst/
reveal	/rɪˈviːl/

English you need

- Gossip

Hey, you'll never guess what I heard.

I heard that they've just got engaged.

You won't believe this, but Marty's got a job.

A little bird told me.

Have you heard about Kate and Darren?

Apparently, they had a big argument.

Don't tell anyone, though!

I won't say a word.

Other words

- Nouns

crash	/kræʃ/
handset	/ˈhændset/
proverb	/ˈprɒvɜːb/
rubber	/ˈrʌbə/
shock	/ʃɒk/
single parent	/ˈsɪŋgl ˈpeərənt/
sole	/səʊl/
youngster	/ˈjʌŋstə/

- Verbs

drop	/drɒp/
groom	/gruːm/
hitchhike	/ˈhɪtʃhaɪk/
save (to buy something)	/seɪv/

- Adjectives

delighted	/dɪˈlaɪtɪd/
missing	/ˈmɪsɪŋ/

- Expressions

in the news	/ɪn ɵə njuːz/
sooner or later	/ˈsuːnə ɔː ˈleɪtə/

Irregular verbs

Infinitive	Past simple	Past participle	Infinitive	Past simple	Past participle
be	was/were	been	lay	laid	laid
beat	beat	beaten	learn	learnt/learned	learnt/learned
become	became	become	leave	left	left
begin	began	begun	let	let	let
bite	bit	bitten	lose	lost	lost
break	broke	broken	make	made	made
bring	brought	brought	mean	meant	meant
build	built	built	meet	met	met
buy	bought	bought	pay	paid	paid
catch	caught	caught	put	put	put
choose	chose	chosen	read	read	read
come	came	come	ride	rode	ridden
cost	cost	cost	ring	rang	rung
cut	cut	cut	run	ran	run
do	did	done	say	said	said
draw	drew	drawn	see	saw	seen
dream	dreamt/dreamed	dreamt/dreamed	sell	sold	sold
drink	drank	drunk	send	sent	sent
drive	drove	driven	shoot	shot	shot
eat	ate	eaten	show	showed	shown
fall	fell	fallen	shut	shut	shut
feed	fed	fed	sing	sang	sung
feel	felt	felt	sink	sank	sunk
fight	fought	fought	sit	sat	sat
find	found	found	sleep	slept	slept
fly	flew	flown	smell	smelt/smelled	smelt/smelled
forget	forgot	forgotten	speak	spoke	spoken
freeze	froze	frozen	spend	spent	spent
get	got	got	stand	stood	stood
give	gave	given	steal	stole	stolen
go	went	gone	swim	swam	swum
grow	grew	grown	take	took	taken
have	had	had	teach	taught	taught
hear	heard	heard	tell	told	told
hide	hid	hidden	think	thought	thought
hit	hit	hit	understand	understood	understood
hold	held	held	wear	wore	worn
keep	kept	kept	win	won	won
know	knew	known	write	wrote	written